ART and STITCHERY
New Directions

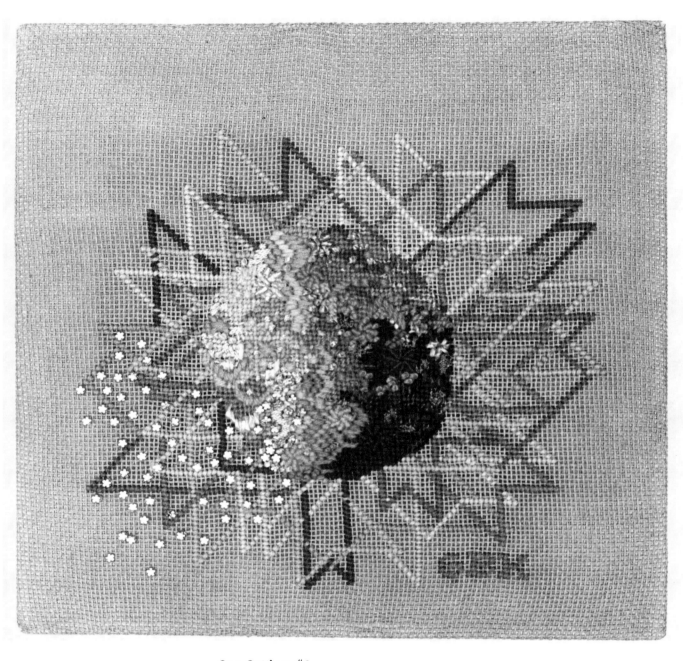

Sun Setting #4
Another interpretation of the sun motif worked on number ten mesh needle-point canvas with straight, tent, spider web stitches and french knots. The colorings are what you might expect of a spectacular sunset, pale yellow, gold, orange scarlet and vermilion. The angular lines shooting out from the circle represent the shimmering, flickering of sun beams. See color section.

ART and STITCHERY
New Directions

Gloria Katzenberg

Charles Scribner's Sons / New York

Library of Congress Cataloging in Publication Data
Katzenberg, Gloria.
    Art and stitchery New Directions
    Bibliography: p.
    1. Embroidery. I. Title.
TT770.K23   746.4'4   73-19284
ISBN 0-684-13765-8

1 3 5 7 9 11 13 15 17 MD/C 20 18 16 14 12 10 8 6 4 2

Printed in the United States of America

Acknowledgements

My warm thanks to all who played a part in the shaping of this book:
Allen Bress for the color photography
Vicki Mitchell for typing the text
My daughter, Susan Katzenberg, for her creative black and white
photographs not just of my work but of natural and man-made wonders
to spark themes for artists everywhere.
My editor, Elinor Parker, for instant feed-back when I asked for
help and advice.

To my husband, Herbert M. Katzenberg who got me through some technical labyrinths and joined me in the quest for images, materials and inspiration that could be found only in odd corners at unexpected times. It took time and patience. He had both.

And to Doria Phelps, my one-month-old granddaughter. . . the future.

Contents

List Of Color Illustrations

to be found after page 48

Preface

Embroidery has grown beyond hearts and flowers, frogs and toad-stools or fool-the-eye furs, marble and malachite while there will always be a place for these. For those dedicated to the textile and stitchery arts, I offer this collection as evidence that deeper ideas and emotion can be expressed just as creatively as in other art forms and emerge as the clearest communication.

The sculptor works in stone, wood, metal and plastic with a specific set of tools. The painter creates by mixing paint and applying it to canvas with brush or palette knife. The potter pounds and manipulates wet clay into shapes and forms. All are involved in the same process and concerned with a common end, the statement of a personal vision, feeling or idea into the reality of form. All are exploring aesthetic problems no matter what the tools, techniques and materials.

When a stitched textile reflects a balance of inspiration, sensibility, sound thinking and interesting materials used in an original way, it can reach the level of fine art.

My emphasis in this book is on personal discovery and the process of creation from the first emotional response to the last design detail. The work is not here to be slavishly reproduced but rather to inspire to new directions and broader, deeper areas of art experience.

ART and STITCHERY
New Directions

Galaxy

Assorted washers attached to black velveteen are combined with horseshoe nails, straight stitches and spider webs to convey shooting stars, planets and anything else up there that we on earth can't be sure of. Tiny clear glass beads add a glitter that one sees on a clear, star-filled night. Only silver metallic thread was used because of the impact of limiting the colors, the sharp contrast between black and silver and again, the sparkle of such a nightscape.

Hangings in Fabric and Thread

Hangings in fabric and thread represent an art form that functioned symbolically in early history in wedding, funeral and triumphal processions while enriching the environment. Hangings also served practical purposes by screening and partitioning and shading sunlit atriums and courtyards. Cold, drab marble and stone walls were warmed, softened and brightened by the addition of embroidered textiles sometimes referred to as the "clothing of architecture". The word "hanging" encompassed everything from large curtains, tent and bed hangings to screens, sails, banners, canopies and valances. Today, embroidered hangings still make marvelous screens, room dividers, and draperies but my focus here is on the creative feeling and vision that can be expressed through fabric and thread with little or no practical purpose other than to exist for its own sake. If a work serves both ends, all the better. I draw from the past with respect but venture to create an art form that mixes media and techniques and reflects the spirit, sensibility, taste and discovery of our own age.

DEFINITION OF EMBROIDERY

Embroidery is stitches on any material in order to add a creative dimension to it. A highly textured and sensuous art form, embroidery is appealing to the eye as well as the touch. Of great age, it has always been dynamic and continues to grow provocatively in fascinating directions. Today stitched art is teamed up with new images that reflect the atmosphere and cultural climate of the times and emerge as a compelling form of creative expression. Sometimes called "stitchery" because the word connotes a contemporary feeling, embroidery can have the same evocative powers as painting, sculpture, graphic and other art forms. There is, in fact, so much borrowing back and forth of techniques and materials that the borderlines between them are dissolving. Different types of embroidery, crewel, needlepoint, drawn work, needleweaving, appliqué, quilting, etc . . . can be freely combined in a single work.

Exercise with soft drink can tops and screen
A slice of screening is couched on smooth, closely woven, black wool fabric and is echoed in four floating embroidered fragments worked in straight silver threaded stitches. The can top pulls are today's image and fascinating to play with. The design is a start of, or the end of, a stark, dramatic design, all silver and black.

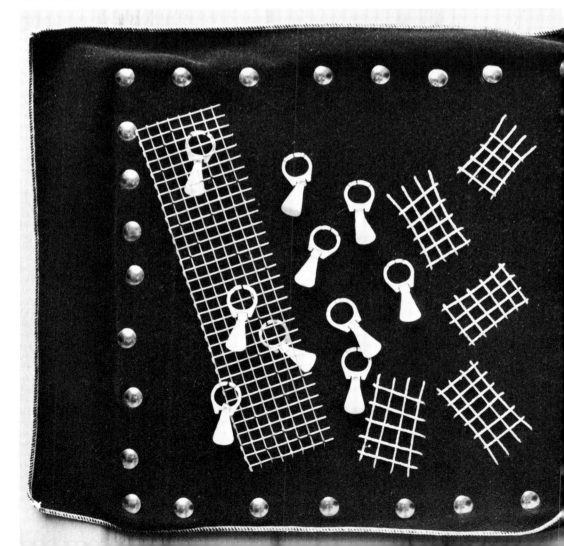

Space Flower

Way-out flower in moon landscape colors, grays and silver, is laid out on deep black-purple wool background fabric. The flower heads are cut out areas that are woven over with the needle in a web-like pattern. Roller skate parts are threaded through the largest cut out to represent growth and attract the eye to the area of greatest importance. The stems are worked in herringbone stitches in silver metallic, wool and angora threads.

Exercise in padding shapes
Triangles, rectangles and circles are stuffed with batting and then embroidered around the edges and on top in different ways. Notice the fascinating shadows thrown by the high rise shapes as well as the stitches and threads.

Still another name for today's embroidery is "soft art" and it includes any work made of pliable materials that is stitched. A recent exhibition featured work made of materials originally designed for commercial purposes: rope, cording, piping, felt, chiffon, foam, latex, string, vinyl and gauze. The artists recycled and transformed the materials into creative images. Some of the work included stitchery. It was padded, stuffed, inflated, tied, draped, knotted, gathered, woven, dyed, silkscreened, painted and photo blue-printed. In the England of James I, and earlier on the Continent, embroidery was stuffed, padded and worked in the round, assuming a sculptured look. Strips of flat and corrugated metal were used to represent water and seed pearls, colored beads, glass and feathers were added for enriching effects. While today's use of these techniques and materials marks a revival rather than a discovery, the form it takes is fresh and relevant to this time.

Used up typewriter ribbon, recycled
Red and black ribbon embellishes open drapery fabric with long and short lengths of turkey-worked stitches that were later slit. Added to this fringed look is a series of straight stitches worked in zigzag fashion.

NEW DIRECTIONS

In England, 1970, an art class of boys and girls were asked to bring parts of discarded machinery to school to see what design ideas could be sparked by the assorted forms. Interesting images arrived: screws, gaskets, car parts, springs, nails, gear rings, clutch plates and ball races. Armed with some design training and minimal embroidery techniques and stitches, the class astonished the teacher

Sunburst #1

The sun is the source of light, growth, warmth but sometimes a force of destruction and drought. It can be wonderful in the form of renewal and terrible in the form of disease in the tropics. Symbolically the sun's light conveys enlightenment and with it the idea of fertility governing the seasons and a good crop. One of the most widely explored art motifs, the sun's circular shape symbolizes eternity as it is an endless movement turning back into itself.

The design is composed around a cut-out circle in the canvas which is backed with highly glossy silver foil paper after all the stitchery is completed. A series of straight stitches is laid out across the opening then whipped round and round until partly covered with silver and gold threads. Uncut loops of turkey work in bright yellow straw are worked in three areas, emphasizing the circular shape of the design. Chain and straight stitches are worked around the circle and tiny tent stitches are scattered like seeds at the top of the design. Turkey work fringe hangs at the base of the design and yellow glass beads are placed in a regular pattern around the circle to add further luster and interest to the concept of the sun image. The silver foil was mounted on homosote first. Over it the embroidered canvas was then stretched and stapled in place.

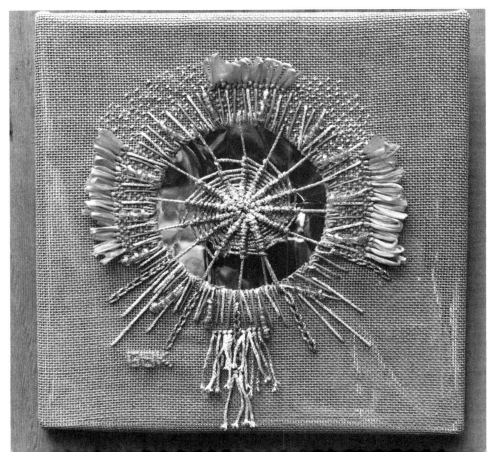

Sunburst #3

The marvelous discarded can top is part rusty, part lustrous, flashing light at the viewer. The roundness is emphasized by the buttonhole stitches around it, but the hanging metallic and wool threads present interesting opposition by their long, linear quality. These are incongruous materials, by some standards, but very much in tune to me. The needlepoint canvas background adds still another dimension as its texture is rough and its structure square and open. There is a rather tongue-in-cheek quality in this combination.

with uninhibited, exciting work. The emphasis was on composition and unbridled "letting go" rather than stitches, thread and classic approaches. Apparently it hardly occurred to the boys that they were embroidering, in the antique sense of the word. Stitching was simply one element of the design and a tool for its realization. Embroidery today is wearing many hats. More and more unusual and unexpected materials are joined to fabric and thread so that it really isn't too surprising to see a rusty can top couched to elegant Thai silk fabric—or needlepoint canvas. The range of

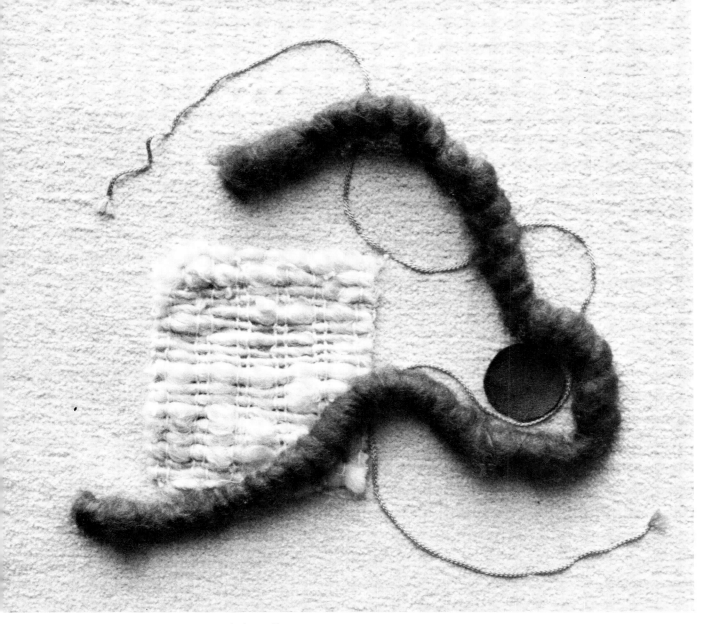

Fabric collage
Handspun heavy wool thread, a scrap of loosely woven fabric, a circle and a thin cord are couched on background fabric.

techniques and mixing of media is as wide as the ideas and stylistic approaches of the artists. Embroidery can be combined with collage and appliqué where fragments of other fabrics or paper are superimposed on background fabric in overlapping arrangements. They might cover the background completely or exist as a few forms in the center. These fragments might also be hand woven, knitted, crocheted, hooked and macraméd. Their edges would affect the character of the design, whether clean cut, frayed, torn to get freer forms or singed to achieve a dark, curled edge.

MIXED MEDIA AND TECHNIQUES

Padded or stuffed embroidery gains a third dimension and can be hung freely or stand on its own. It may be studded with small accents of wood, glass or hand-made ceramic beads. An embroidered design may call for a hole or slit to be made in the fabric. The hole then becomes as meaningful a design shape as a solid mass. It can be decoratively stitched in many ways: woven over, with beads threaded through it, stitched around to secure cut edges as well as draw attention or backed with either another

Cut-out area in fabric

A definitive shape is created by cutting into the background fabric. Here the opening is stitched with buttonhole to secure the cut edges and long stitches weave over the cut-out in more interesting shapes which are quite irregular and open. Infinite possibilities are open to the inventive; another color could be backed against the hole, beads or other materials could be added, another stitched motif might be laid behind the hole, and so on.

color or stitched motif. The hole becomes an area of dominant interest, luring the eye to some mystery behind. Sometimes many slits are made in the background fabric and different color fabrics are attached behind, as many as six to eight, so that layers of colors vibrate through the openings. Discarded soft materials are used as major images in embroidered design. One artist designed around an old coat using it as a symbol to memorialize her father. Another combined stitches with the memorabilia of a bygone era, one for which she felt a special nostalgia. The mixing of media, including recycled material, is intriguing not only because of the challenges posed but because each medium expresses a unique sensation. A well-done work taking this into account and keeping it under control can be expressive of many compelling sensations. Scrap will have one effect, driftwood another, surgical tubing and soiled rope off the street, still another.

The sewing machine is an accepted creative tool today, capable of producing interesting linear design effects. It is equipped to stitch through multilayers of fabric in order to quilt, enrich padded

Close up of Under the Spreading . . .
Detail of hole cut into fabric with wooden beads and threads stretched over it. See color section.

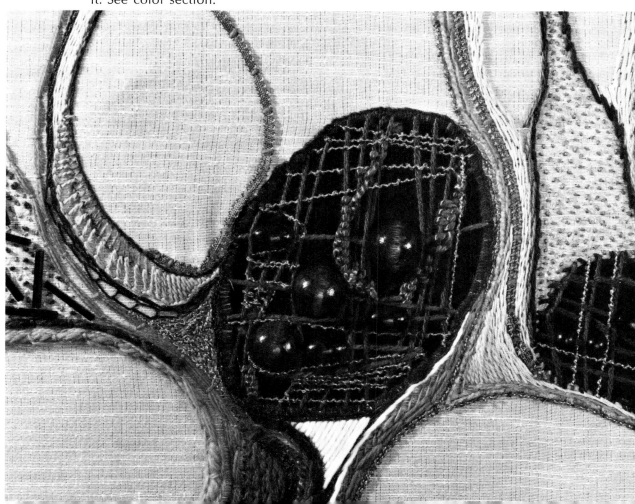

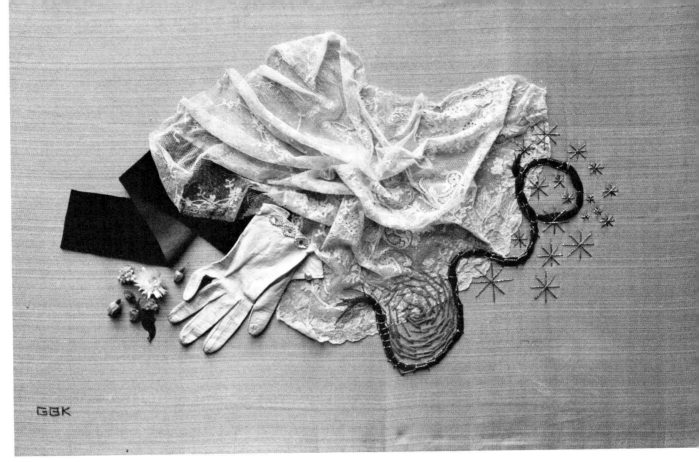

Soft Sounds

There is a tongue-in-cheek wistfulness about this collage. The lace from my mother's wedding dress is softly draped to accentuate its delicacy. The white glove seems to go with lace, velvet and rose buds. The flowers are from dried English potpourri and are glued on, then sprayed to preserve them. A heavy purple thread, suggestive of majesty, formality and dignity is couched with a wide chain in lavender metallic thread. Star motifs are added to symbolize the excitement and sparkle of dress up, as it once was. There is an extraordinarily textural variation that is not overdone. The background fabric is a subtle blend of the colors of the design.

forms and attach appliquéd shapes. Tie-dyed, spot-bleached, paint-spattered, printed and patterned fabrics are embroiderable. In these instances, there are images already on the fabric that must be considered decoratively. They might be accented, highlighted and outlined; each addition, however, must be a meaningful and relevant one. Patterned and busy background fabrics are more difficult to work with because of competition between design already present and design to be added. One could overpower the other so that both are cancelled out.

ART AND STITCHERY

12

Tracks

Heavily textured, partly open-weave linen fabric is slit across the center, then woven over with wool and linen threads to hold it together as well as embellish it. Small beads are threaded over the open area. Rich brown wood forms are stitched randomly around the base of the design. Sheaf stitches surround these forms and provide an interesting flat echo. There is an interplay between open, close, and high, low relief, all of which animates the design. Earlier phase of the design seemed lacking so I elaborated.

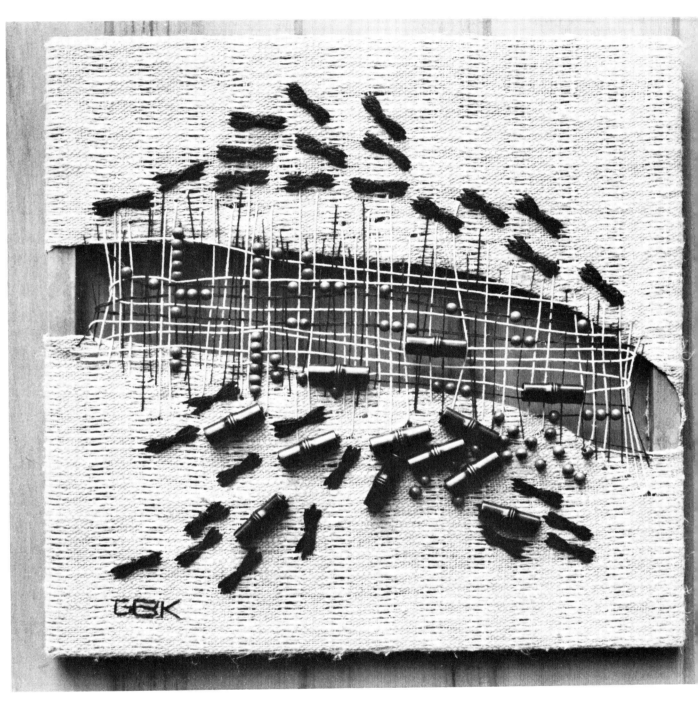

New Images
An assemblage of possible images to team up with fabric and thread, skate parts, washers, wood knobs, a rusty piece of scrap and a cut-out disc. They have diverse shapes, tonal differences, qualities of high and flat and sheen and matte. The scrap reflects no light; the rest do in varying amounts.

While stitchery successfully fuses with other art forms and incorporates materials and objects not necessarily heretofore associated with it, it should not totally surrender its identity. What it borrows should be applicable and this, of course, is controversial. Some will quibble with certain combinations, others may be purist and deride anything added to embroidery that isn't stitch or thread. For me, the only issue is that there be analogy between object, thread, stitch and fabric, each a fitting addition to the design. It is valid to use an object for shock value but not for strictly exhibitionism. Your objective may be to reflect a distaste, a political protest or simply a witticism. Since these materials and objects are the products of our culture, they tell a relevant story in an immediate way.

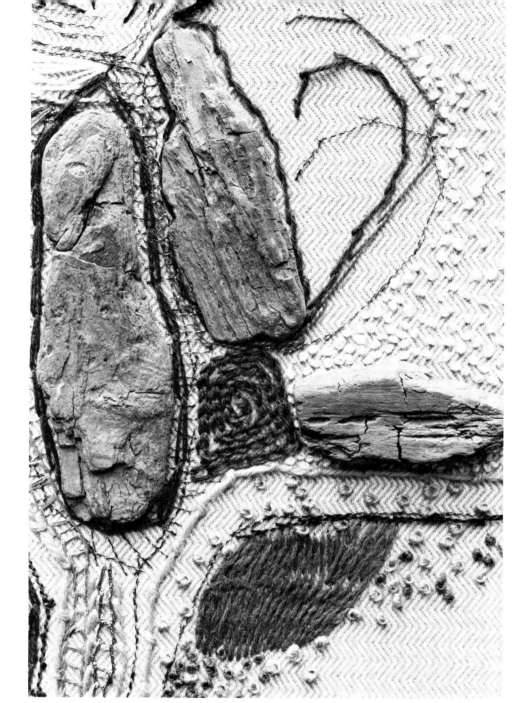

Close up of Wood Weathered
Time-worn, weather-etched wood provides a textured, sculptured look to the collaged design. The wood is the focal point of the composition. Note herringbone patterned wool background fabric and how it works with design. See color section.

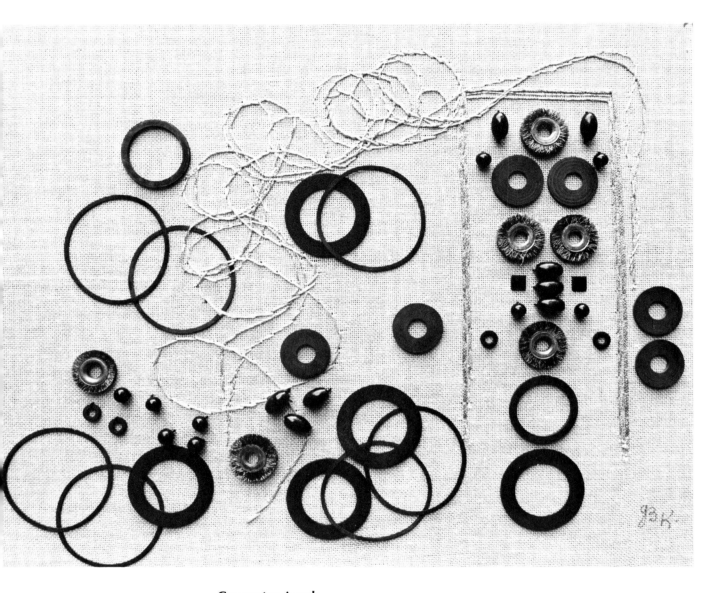

Computer Amok
Variously sized rubber cut-outs and washers are arranged in orderly fashion on the right side of the design to emphasize the working computer contrasted to the left side where everything has gone awry. The wires are tangled and finally hang limply at the bottom of the work. They emanate from the right side or the computer so there is a connection. Some wooded and plastic beads are used to simulate dials and knobs. Some have a lustrous quality, others are rather flat, some are high rise, others are flatter. The color scheme is black, gold and silver, closely resembling the colors of machinery. The design is worked on even weave fabric that was pre-stretched.

Computer Amok . . . final phase
The design stopped here for a while until I felt the need to go on; something about it seemed unfinished, unresolved, yet I was uncertain. After a hiatus of a week, I knew where I wanted to go. The design seemed to gain some depth and interest as I added more threads, some of which dangled off the work limply.

Ocean
Another timeless image that will always inspire the artist, the ever-changing patterns of ebb, flow, billow and surge are evident here. Foam washing over rocks, scalloping forms against the sand, cresting breakers in various phases of development are endlessly enchanting to watch and draw from.

DESIGN SOURCES

Design is where you find it . . . where it has always been, if you will start looking sensitively at the world around and within you in a closer way. Designing requires being attuned to the whole environment, looking inside things, at the spaces between them and their relationships with adjacent things. Pay heed to all your visual experiences and jot down impressions, a memorable color scheme, a whimsical contour, a good composition. Remember that they all reduce to lines, shapes, forms, colors, and textures.

Composition On Beach
I arranged rotting wood, dried sea weed, shells and the fruit of an exotic plant on the sand. My aim was to blend tones, rough with smooth surfaces and contrasting shapes and forms for future designing. This is a still life to which I can refer at any time for infinite ideas.

Swash

A mini view of the ebb of a breaker or perhaps a little pool of water left by a wave with the flotsam of pebbles, sand etc. Whites, blues and blue greens in wool, cotton and metallic are worked in stem, chain and turkey work stitches. The background fabric is loosely woven, open drapery material. The smooth rounded pebbles are held on the fabric with glue.

Wheel
The radiating spokes lead the eye of the viewer to the center or hub and back out to the outer circle which holds the form together visually. The repetition of the spokes establishes interest and rhythm in the design.

Design can be wrought from the window patterns of a skyscraper or the twist of a pretzel. Notice the way the sun drenches the side-walk and shadow dances where light has fled. Study the structure of a watch works, the geometric façade of computers, the shapes of your furnace room. A sump pump can be inspiring if you look beyond its function to the essence of its form. Almost anything is designable and embroiderable.

Homage to Circles

A long strip of cut-out rigid plastic scrap and perforated soft plastic ribbon set the design scene with circular motifs which are then echoed by button-hole stitches worked in the round. The plastic scrap is attached to the fabric with lots of tiny straight stitches. The added circles are worked in different weights of threads: crewel wool, linen and cotton. The color scheme was kept subdued: black, navy, royal blue, blue gray, shades of lighter grays and a range of off-whites. The darker circles are placed at the bottom of the design to give the base some weight. The background is a natural colored linen.

Arch
The curve of the arch sharply contrasts with the geometry of the black iron gate which is echoed intriguingly by another arch behind, filled with bright light. The worn cobblestones are irregular and so provide another contrast to the rigid design of the iron. The cobbles are rough, the iron is smooth; it is an inspiring scene for design. Observe also the many differences in tones, from white to grays and finally, black.

APPROACHES TO DESIGNING

My approach to designing is spontaneous rather than academic. A famous writer views it this way.

"Theorise, theorise all you like—but when you start . . . go for it with instinct and intuition."*

I usually create expressionistically as I stitch along, the way some artists used to drip paint on canvas. I am moved and motivated by the materials at hand, taking cues directly from them. I never do extensively detailed drawing or coloring beforehand and my work changes often from the first path taken, as intuition and instinct interact with the stimuli of materials. At every stage, I stand back and examine, compare and weigh one design element against another, checking craftsmanship which must be impeccable. Since materials act as catalyst to creative ideas, you should examine fabrics to understand the structure and weave which are its character, taking all this into account as the background for your design. Whether it is loosely, tightly woven, of nubby or smooth fibers, shiny or matte, opaque or sheer, colored or muted; all will affect what you can do with it. Literally hundreds of design thoughts will be sparked at this moment. Threads can be tossed against the fabric to see if there is mere congeniality or true excitement and other materials and objects can be tested at this important moment in the evolution of self expression.

Sometimes I draw a few light colored guidelines with a waterproof felt marking pen to place forms or a contour on the fabric. The finished embroidery is the elaboration of this rough sketching. Design should fill the space allotted to it; it can be perfectly centered or asymmetrical. There ought not to be too much space left at the sides, or top and bottom. A first design should be a simple exercise and considered as part of, but separate from, the background fabric. The most spontaneous expression comes when you

* The Creative Process, Brewster Ghiselin, Mentor Books, New York, 1955.

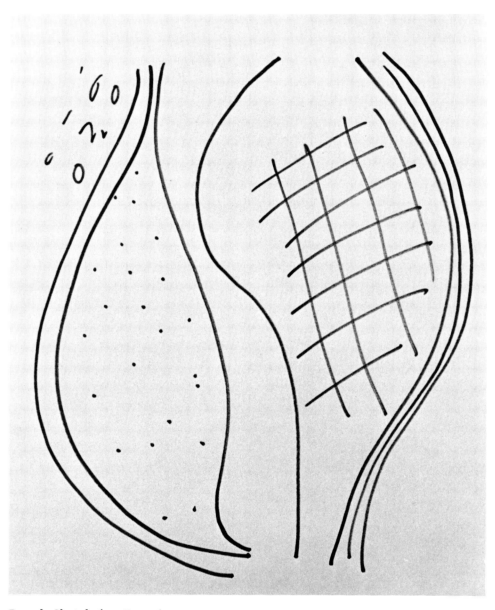

Rough Sketch for Greening

The vaguest outlines of the forms I wanted are sketched here to guide me in the stitching. I referred to the study only at the start, developing the design fully as I proceeded with stitches, threads, colors and other materials. The dots on the left were represented later by beads. See color section.

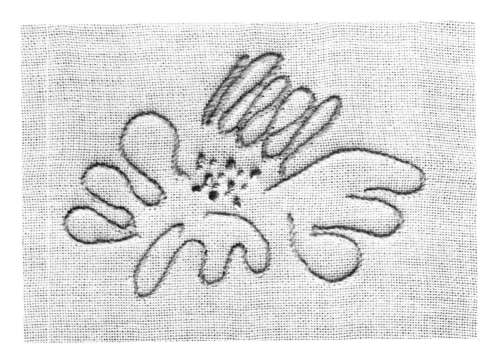

Hint of Flower

Four very curved lines surrounding a central mass of french knots create the suggestion of a slightly abstract flower. This is a bare beginning of design and a simple expression of form that can be shaped into a more elaborated statement.

simply stitch freely all over, as you feel moved, and is my favorite way of working. This is not to say that thought and plan are altogether removed. As suggested earlier, from stage to stage there are intervals of reconsidering and some planning, even ripping out. Everything ever seen, felt and believed, re-emerges in self expression. Once the inspiration has occurred, momentum gathers, one idea leading to the next. All approaches are valid and can climax in the same rewarding moment. What matters is to find the most comfortable and natural way for you.

What is art . . . how does design begin? One writer described it this way.

"Creation begins typically with a vague, even a confused excitement, some sort of yearning, hunch . . ."*

* op. cit.

Scribblings

Swirling, broken, geometric lines make the shapes of design just to open trains of creative thought. A little practice with felt pen scribbling builds confidence and helps you to envision forms overlapping, lines crossing and the look of a stitch on paper. Try drawing in a casual fashion on newspaper and explore line, shape and form freely.

Study For Aromatica

This is a very rough sketch of the barest outline of the much more elaborated design seen in color section. Details were added and changes occurred at every stage. I used black felt markers on ordinary bond paper and worked out my colors expressionistically as I went along in the working of the embroidery. The rich color scheme is touched off by the color of spices which is earthy and muted. The floating, couched threads above the circular forms represent fragrances wafting out of the spices. A few glass beads were added to symbolize the sparkle, smell or taste of something spicy. The background fabric is quite textured, almost nubby.

EMBROIDERY DESIGN

Design has to do with putting things together. As a writer uses words to express feelings and ideas, the designer uses lines and color. Embroidery design is concerned with selecting, arranging and organizing of lines, shapes, forms, colors and textures into an arresting state of balance through stitches. It begins with line which attracts the eye, luring it around as it crosses and divides other lines. Shapes emerge where lines intersect and enclose. Where line stops, the eye also stops, often at an important area of interest in the composition. Line can be straight, undulating, broken, continuous, interlacing, delicate, bold. It underscores, accents,

Human Form
Simplified, slightly distorted thread rendering of the human form worked
directly on open linen. Follow through with many similar exercises, making
needle and thread do your bidding. When you achieve a design that pleases
you, add more detail as you feel confident.

heightens, emphasizes and establishes direction. Line creates form, encloses and fills shape and represents objects. To give importance to a shape, use a heavy or dark thread or bold textured stitches.

When you depict a pictorial theme in stitchery, don't render every detail. Interpret it and simplify it. Distort it if you wish but convey more than the image; get to the feeling behind it. In the human form, for example, omit the features and emphasize the form, changing it a bit. Design can be realistically drawn but embroidery is not meant to produce camera-like reflection. The subject is given new form as it appears to the inner eye of the artist. The usual visual signposts that identify an object are left out. There may be an allusion to it, however subtle. Abstract art focuses on the essence of things, their inherent quality or a symbol that represents it. A symbol is a sort of sign that stands for something else like the circle which conveys eternity, the eagle, power, the cross, Christianity. A symbol can awaken memories, stir emotions and point beyond itself to deeper levels and vistas. A truly abstract design contains an unrecognizable subject. The viewer may see only the color or the texture that is the essence of the subject. The design may be a witty idea or a deeply felt mood of the creator.

Detail of Knot Hole

This is the center portion and focal point of the design showing the appliquéd printed fragment against raw silk. Threads are lacily woven over the fragment and chain stitches surround it. Beads, large and small, reflect dots of highlight and repeat the small round shapes in the print. There is an abundance of surface vitality evident. See KNOTHOLE (p. 35.)

Technological Tangle

Deliberately blurred photograph of telephone wires and equipment (left) offers shapes and forms separated by lines and different tones for the inspired designer. There is a mix here of geometric shapes and the curve of wires surrounding them. Photo courtesy of Robert M. Goldman.

Railroad Tie
There is much here to inspire design: texture of wood, softly curving linear patterns and the dark shapes of the holes and openings in the tie which are important design forms in themselves.

Since things need not look like what they are, abstract art is less restrictive and implies more freedom of approach and rendering. It springs more directly from the mood and emotions of its creator. Whatever the subject matter, it should be significant, have emotional appeal and pique the curiosity of the viewer.

Although I often urge the abandon of rules, I understand the importance of knowing them first. Rules are helpful guidelines that set boundaries and let the designer know what he can achieve. I urge you not to let the rules be inhibiting and restrictive to invention and experiment. Master the techniques of meticulous craftsmanship. Successful design brings into focus the most important part of the scheme, getting all other elements to mesh together

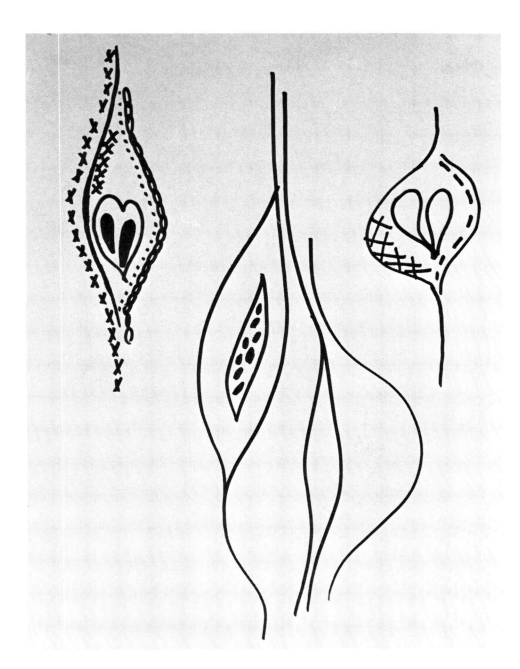

Sketches for Knot hole

Casual outlines of natural forms are shown here with some suggestion of
possible stitches. They can be related to many of the designs in the book, they
are so basic. This is meant to be helpful in guiding you to see how many
creative ideas spark from one form.

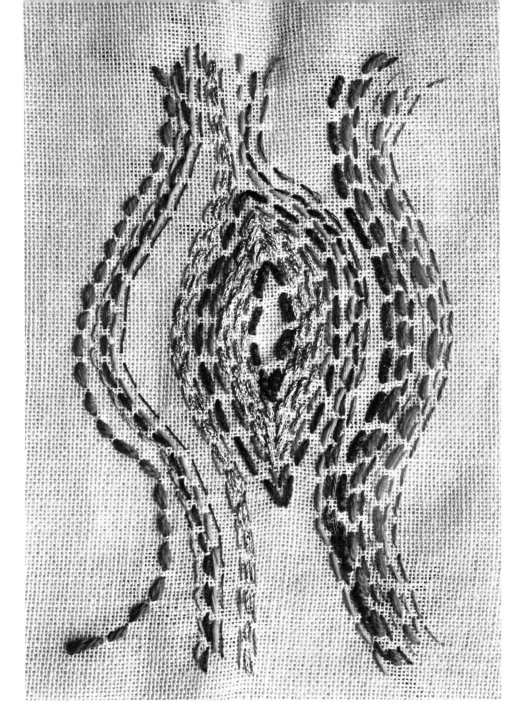

Knot hole exercise

Worked completely in running stitches with thick, thin, wool, cotton, metallic threads, this is a simple design that serves as a starting point. The curving linear forms are graceful and convey the movement of nature and growth. There is interesting contrast through threads and colors and the surface comes alive through reflection of the gold metallic threads which catch the light. The background fabric is moderately open weave natural linen. Railroad ties could be considered inspiration for the shape of this exercise.

in balance and harmony. There is a sense of rightness when the work is finished. Stand back often to see the fullest view of the whole as well as its parts. One more detail at this point and the balance is upset. Experience helps to recognize this moment.

Knot hole

This design, worked on an elegant raw silk fabric, is an interpretation of shapes, forms and the textures of bark and knot holes. A small cut-out of printed linen is appliquéd in the center of the design to achieve depth and dimension as well as contrast with the stitched areas. The colors are quite monochromatic: pale tan, putty, taupe, camel and brown with accents of white and metallic brown.

Knot hole is an elaboration or another more complex interpretation of the running stitch exercise for KNOT HOLE and RAILROAD TIE.

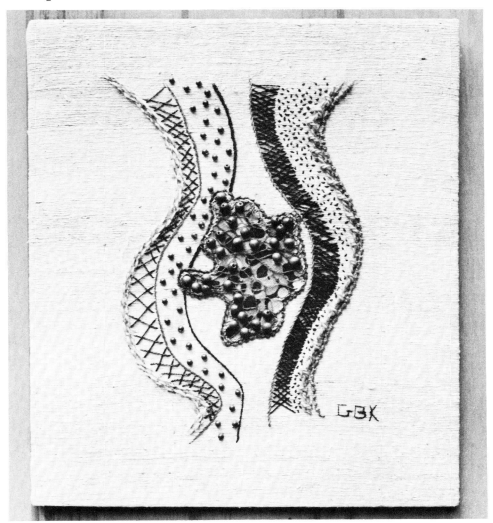

MATERIALS AND TOOLS

Depth and vitality are introduced to design through textural and color contrasts, light and dark, rough and smooth, luster and matte, curly and straight, static and gyrating, bold and wispy.

Design decisions are like those you make daily and are affected by personal exposure, bias, tastes, imagination and daring. All self-expression is a fusion of these factors which in a sense are being shaken up and set down in a new form. Choices and changes are made at every stage with frequent flashes of insight that spur you on. If you bog down, stop and turn your back for a day or so. A fresh glimpse will do wonders for inspiration. Whatever tools, techniques and materials you draw from, it is the idea that counts. It represents your way of visualizing, feeling and expressing.

I repeatedly stress the importance of alluring fabrics as a stimulus to design ideas. Collect all you can and accept any offerings from friends. Haunt the nearby outlets to build the stockpile that will keep your mind teeming with ideas and images. Accumulate all types: sheers, nubby, open weave, smooth close weave, pile, patterned, printed, transparent, tweeded, twilled, assorted colors and muted, neutrals. Make your own discoveries by trial stitching on patches of variously structured fabrics. Notice that a stitch on velveteen sinks in and gets lost in the pile and how pattern in the background fabric affects the stitches. Muted, even weaves in linen, cotton and wool make good backgrounds to design. I suggest, in general, working on good quality fabrics. They have more character and endure longer.

Needlepoint canvas size 16 to 5 meshes per inch can be used much like any other fabric. It is starched and has evenly spaced meshes or holes that usually are meant to be covered thoroughly with counted stitches. I suggest using the tan color and leaving unworked areas to play up its interesting character. Use a blunt tip tapestry needle that fits the meshes and allows easy passage of thread. Tape or stitch all cut edges to prevent ravels and snagging of working thread.

Linen, fine, coarse, open, close weave

Left to right: open mesh glass fabric, sheer voile, opaque wool fabric, open mesh heavy linen-cotton

Cotton: Muslin, ticking, monk's cloth, sail cloth, percale
Wool
Rayon
Silk
Jute
Velveteen
Organdy, Chiffon, Voile
Synthetics, dacron, nylon
Chicken Wire
Fiberglass Screening
Flannel
Netting
Felt
Used Onion and Vegetable Bags
Old Burlap Bags
Antique Fabrics either as background or for collage fragments
Corduroy

The quest for materials will sharpen your visual awareness and you are bound to learn important things about their inherent possibilities. Acquire threads the same way. Look in the back of art and craft magazines for ads on handspun and dyed threads. Visit weaving and yarn shops and pick up diverse types. In addition to traditional crewel, tapestry, persian, cotton, rayon and linen threads, there are knotted, looped, bulky, spot-dyed, uneven and slubbed threads:

metallic, non-tarnishable
chenille, twine, cord, rope, string
raffia
bouclé
mohair
angora
braid

Some threads are too thick or nubby to thread into needle and fabric. They are often such exciting fibers that you will want to make creative use of them. These threads can be attached to fabric by a technique called couching. Even the most humble shoe lace, ribbon from a gift package or typewriter ribbon can be elevated to an important role in design.

Close up of Renascence
Thick, thin, fuzzy, smooth, shiny threads are superimposed on evenly woven canvas, each contributing to the interest of the others. See color section.

Detail of Cycling

The shape of the design resulted from the natural way the wire spread itself, with a prod here and there from me. All the materials have a particularly lustrous quality. The wire is ultra reflective, dazzling the eye; the metallic thread has sheen and sparkle, and the amber glass beads have a translucent character. Even the elegant silk fabric has a shiny surface. The only stich used is turkey work or rya. This produced the random lengths of fringe. The color scheme is almost monochrome. See color section.

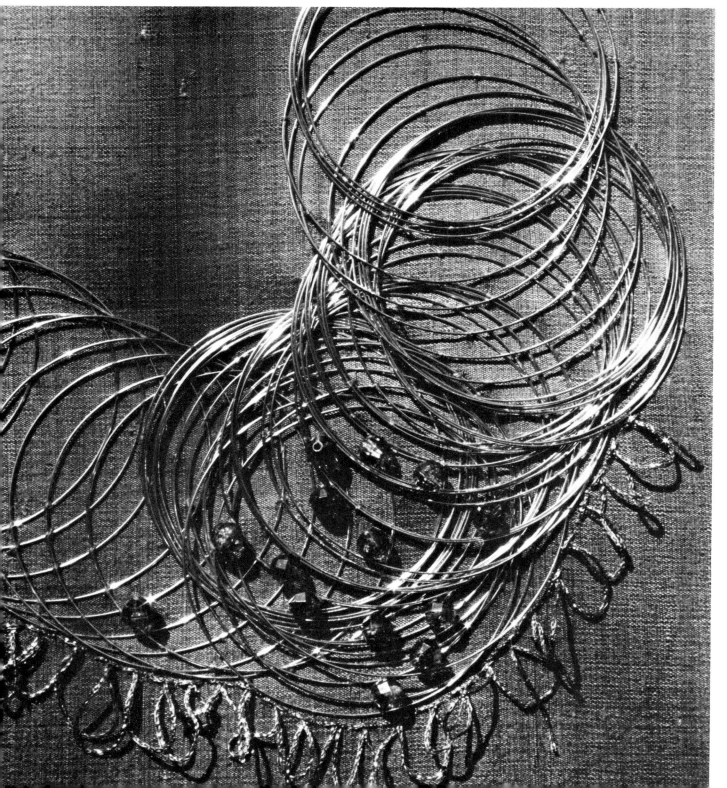

There are less obvious materials like surgical tubing, leather strips, plastic tubing, rubber strips, foil and perforated ribbon. Then there are **the natural materials:**

    shells
    pods
    seeds
    weathered wood
    feathers
    pebbles
    coral
    dried plants and flowers
    nuts

Paul Klee collected molluscs, lichens, sea urchins, crystals, mica and coral to study their structure and Jean Dubuffet made collages of butterflies.

Manufactured materials and objects of interest:

    every variety of bread—glass, wood, ceramic, plastic
    sequins
    paillettes
    wood shapes, knobs, etc.
    buttons
    plastic rings
    plexiglass forms
    shisha glass
    washers
    gaskets
    nails
    metal shavings
    copper and aluminum wire
    skate parts
    foil papers
    scouring pads
    hair nets
    corrugated cardboard

I recently saw a fascinating design stitched around a bicycle sprocket. Scrap can be captivating in combination with stitches when well conceived. Twentieth century sculpture couldn't exist without the scrap material which tells our technology story so well. In the right setting, used wire, bits of discarded steel, the rusty top of a soup can remerges as a tour de force in design. It often has a symbolic meaning, losing its original identity once incorporated into design. Once again, I suggest caution to avoid a contrived result. There should be a sense of rightness and analogy between materials. An attached object must never be too heavy for its fabric background so that it pulls it out of shape. I consider it valid to use glue to augment stitches or instead of them. Check out the perishability of objects as they may not be worthy of your time. I do spray dried natural materials with Blair or Krylon to preserve them. The needle is the link between design, thread, stitch and fabric. Have some of every kind and size at hand. It saves time.

Crewel: short, sharp, with long slender eyes for easy threading, size 1 to 10

Chenille: short shaft, large eyes for thicker threads, sizes 18 to 22

Tapestry: blunt tip, large eye, size 13 to 24 (lower number is largest needle)

Bead Needle: very long, slender shaft, tiny eye for fine silk thread to thread into fine beads. A threader may be necessary.

Other useful tools:

Tailor's chalk for marking guidelines on dark colors

Felt tip marking pens in light colors waterproof and permanent (test them)

Straight pins to secure a heavy thread before couching

Swingline stapler #101, to staple fabric on a stretcher frame

Sobo or Elmer's Glue—dries a clear color and holds eternally

Stretcher frames, hoops, assorted sizes are useful and necessary to prevent puckers and distortion due to the tension of stitching

Magnifying glass—for enlarging design detail

Fine sewing silk for attaching beads and sequins

Embroidery scissors and large shears

Blair, spray fix, dries quickly to a matte finish, protects dried flowers, newspaper, might prevent discoloration and brittle-ness

Homosote Board, for mounting finished stitchery

Masonite, another choice for mounting completed work

Once you have conceived a design, consider where it will hang. Will it be seen against wood, marble, stone or plaster? Will it be clearly visible or somewhat shaded in a long, narrow, dark hall? To check out shape and scale, cut a piece of newspaper and hold it against the wall. Perhaps the area would benefit from a huge square or a circular shape. Or possibly a long narrow piece best fits the location. Color and scale must be in tune with the setting. Back off frequently, as what seems bold while you work tends to recede from afar. Always cut your background fabric on the straight, leaving four or five inches all around for stretching, mount-ing and blocking, if necessary.

Stitch or bind cut edges with one-inch masking tape to contain ravels. Be sure your fabric is clean and freshly ironed. Wrap it over a stretcher-frame bought at the art supply store at a nominal price

Materials
Crewel, persian, rayon, bouclé, pearl cotton, silk, metallic tweed blend, metallic, sewing silk and linen threads are combined here with beads, wood knobs, a large embroidery hoop and scissors attached to a ribbon for easy access.

Assorted wooden frames: stretchers and embroidery hoops

and staple at one inch intervals, pulling tightly and evenly as you secure it. The fabric can also be thumb-tacked to the frame but eventually it would have to be re-stretched anyway. A taut fabric supports stitches; it keeps a neat unpuckered surface. Another advantage of stapling to start with is that the finished work need not have a picture frame added unless you want one. It can be hung as is. Very sheer materials and needlepoint canvas will look better if lined. Just staple the lining first, then staple the embroidered fabric over it, on the same stretcher-frame.

With fabric ready to go, assemble threads with attention to color, texture and tonal contrasts. Think about stitches and techniques with which to carry out your design. It is a good idea to work where you can see all sorts of materials for the ideas and impetus they feed you as you work.

There are a few tricks that aid the novice in arriving at a design. Shapes can be cut out of gray-toned or multi-colored tissue paper and moved around the fabric like musical chairs. When the composition strikes you as arresting, pin the shapes down, and trace lightly around them. Two overlapped shapes produce a third shape and another color. Instead of cutting shapes, try tearing to get a freer form and more ragged edge. The gray-toned paper gives a marvelous tonal variation that you might never have arrived at by yourself, from pure white to inky black with many grays between.

Another trick is to spill a drop or two of acrylic paint or ink on a sheet of paper and blow it carefully around into rivulets of shapes and forms. Or, having spilled ink, scratch it around the paper with a tiny twig to get creative happenings. The well-known ink blot can be the start of an expressive stitchery. Fold a sheet of paper, then open it; spill a few drops of ink down the fold line. Gently re-fold the paper, pressing the folded edges together to force the ink spill outward in lines, masses and intriguing forms. Copy, trace and transfer all resultant designs on fabric, then develop and shape as the power of invention moves you. You may be surprised and pleased by the turns your design will take and how differently it will finalize from its original idea. I don't suggest that it will be artistic nirvana, though it could be, but rather a means to an end, an approach that may be helpful.

Spilled ink blown around paper into chance designs and patterns

Cut and torn paper

Cut out and torn pieces of construction paper are arranged in a design composition. They are rubber-cemented to a sheet of light-toned construction paper. The torn pieces differ from those that are cut in the character of their edges. The torn fragments have a more free, raggedy form while the cut-outs are tight, smooth, even-edged. The same effects can be captured with textiles.

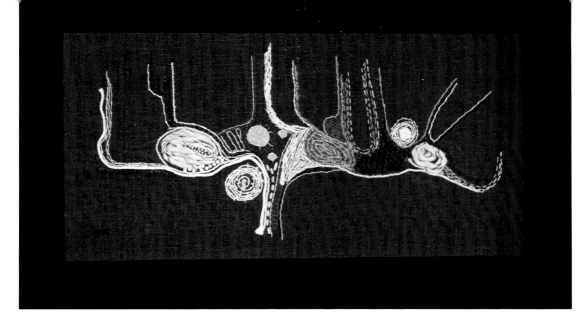

Espalier

An interpretation of a shrub interestingly trained against a wall, as in photo opposite. This is worked on very rough, bright red linen. The color scheme is white, off white, silver metallic, pale gray, medium and dark gray, black. The threads are angora, wool, linen, cotton and rayon. There is a sensation of upward growth from a central stalk or stem which is reinforced with small wood beads. A few sequins underline one of the worms, some black beads fill a shape and add necessary texture. There is a particular grace and upward mobility in the espalier form. Couching, stem stitches are the only stitches used throughout.

Under the spreading . . .

Branch forms reaching upward, variable textures and cut-out areas interplay in this symbolic design which suggests an old poem that I liked. Threads are criss-crossed over the cut-out shapes in the design and large, brown wooden beads are threaded through to suggest the chestnuts. The colors are personal, reds, salmons, bittersweets, tans, browns, putty, white. Stem, seeding, button-hole, chain stitches were used with some french knots in wool, stranded cotton, linen and rayon threads of different weights.

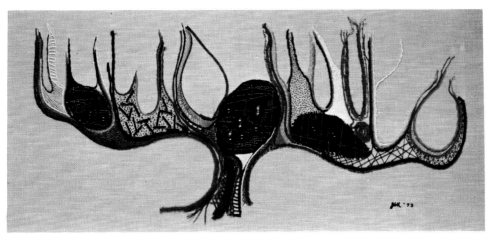

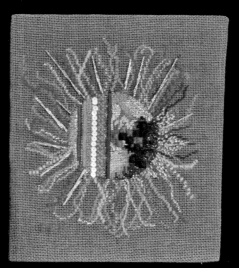

Sunburst #1

The top left design in the photo is described on page 6.

Sunburst #2

The left side of the second design pictured here is filled with rigid geometric lines of straight, tent, van dyke stitches and french knots. There is one row of white opaque sequins. The right side of the design is very freely worked, the same stitches worked in loose arrangement. Pale yellows and golds including metallics are used to represent the early day sun. The colors deepen into russets and copper mixed with dark orange. The metallic threads gyrate like sunbeams and the wavy lines emanating out of the main motif suggest the ever-moving rays of light. The design was worked on light tan needlepoint canvas. See page 62 for detail photo.

Sunburst #3

This version is shaped around the scrapped top of a soup can. Buttonhole stitches and turkey work are combined in the design work on tan needlepoint canvas. See page 7 for description.

Sun Setting #4

Another interpretation of the sun motif worked on number ten mesh needle-point canvas with straight, tent, spider web stitches and french knots. The colorings are what you might expect of a spectacular sunset, pale yellow, gold, orange scarlet and vermilion. The angular lines shooting out from the circle represent the shimmering, flickering of sun beams.

Highly reflective gold beads are added to bring an extra dimension of dazzle and a balancing texture to the raised stitches.

Seismic Event

The stitching is based on needle weaving over foundations of straight stitches laid down on the fabric.

Mauve Majesty

A needlepoint study of color and texture in a geometric design is bordered on the left side by a high pile of turkey work stiches combining all the threads and colors of the flat shapes. Persian wool yarn is combined with lavender metallic thread, balancing shimmer against opaque.

Dissonance

Social protest is expressed with a collage of newspaper fragments that are glued to purple wool fabric. The focal point of the design is the massed bullets of copper, clustered in the center. Straight stitches of scarlet straw project from there out and point to the headlines. Copper metallic thread accents the color of the bullets. Herringbone stitches around the edges of the newspapers hold the design together. The newspaper is sprayed with clear Krylon to preserve it.

Needling

A solidly stitched area of lively colors. There are lacy next to packed close stitches, dense and fragmented color. Herringbone, wide chain, spider web, stem and van dyke stitches combine in this design. Linen twill is the background fabric.

Bonsai

Inspired by the elegant, pruned, miniature garden, this monotone design introduces every green imaginable as well as many types of thread. I tried to get the weeping quality of Japanese specimen plants and the suggestion of upward growth. Green glass beads add a relief contrast and sparkle to the scheme, worked on tan needlepoint canvas and mounted on homosote.

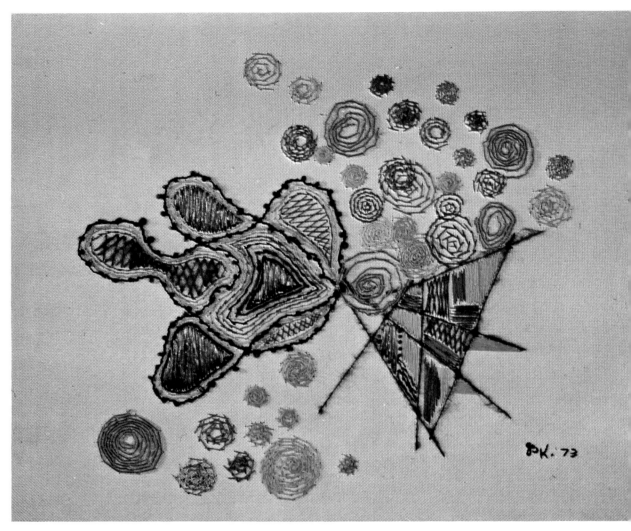

Sky Lab

Inspired by the fascinations of space exploration, this totally subjective version or vision of a vehicle floating in space is worked in straw, chenille, linen, wool and mohair threads. The forms are rather fanciful though the round shapes certainly are symbolic of celestial bodies. There is the contrast between rounds and straights heightened by brilliant purples and greens of many shades. Natural linen is the background of this embroidery created with straight, stem and couched stitches.

Harvest

One stitch expresses the whole theme of this design, the harvesting of wheat and the bundles left standing in the fields. Sheaf stitch worked in a variety of scales and threads and colors is accented and highlighted with amber glass beads which symbolize the dazzle of sunlight on the fields. The background fabric is a rich, medium brown, rough-textured jute that in itself is an interesting contrast to the rather elegant motifs and materials.

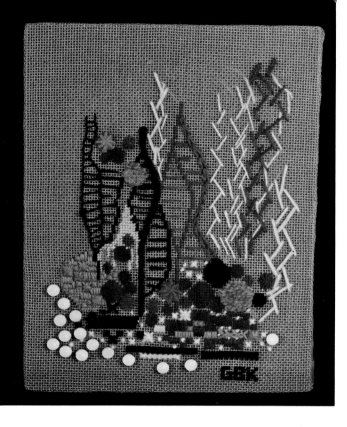

Micro scape
Worked on needlepoint canvas an upward float-ing vegetation is suggested with wide chain stitches. The design is linear with contrasts of some round and zigzag forms at the bottom. Tent and spider web stitches are worked with french knots, smyrna and cross stitches. Chalk-white, faceted opaque glass, beads, suggest flora and fauna of the sea and reflect light.

Wood weathered
Weathered wood fragments are the focal point of this design. French knots are scattered around as a unifying device for all the larger design shapes. The larger knots throw shadows bringing tonal changes to very the surface. Metallic threads en-liven the design and highlight the forms. The frame is old barn wood. See page 15 for detail.

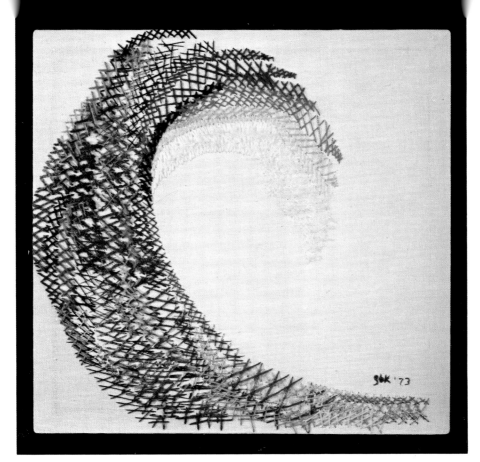

Surge, swell, billow

A spontaneous design which I began with not the foggiest idea of anything but one stitch, the herringbone which I thought I would work simply, building up texture by overlaying stitches and interlacing them. Every type of thread was used: straw, silk, wool, cotton, linen. A thickly textured composition began to emerge and a form seemed to be taking shape. It appeared to be a cresting wave and so I treated it as such. From that point on, I worked with a definite form in mind, ending the wave with a nubby white thread suggestive of foam spraying. A pure, white linen fabric is the background of this design.

Echoes

A fragment of heavy upholstery fabric is appliquéd on tan needlepoint canvas. Smyrna stitches echo the linear design and reverse the echo while eight halfway worked rhodes stitches line up between. The texture and color of the canvas animate this geometric composition. The stitched design is worked in persian wool yarn.

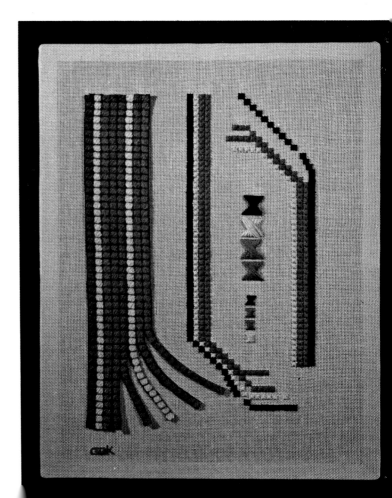

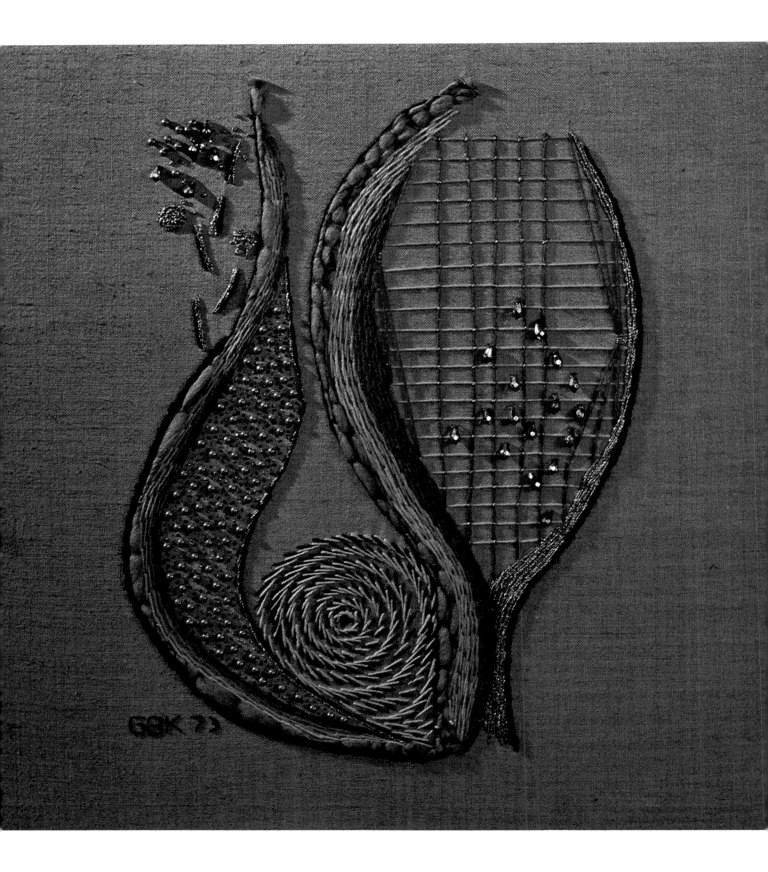

Greening

Shades of green from pale budding to deepest value are worked side by side to achieve the luminescence that parallels the freshness and glow of spring. The iridescent prism-shaped glass beads symbolize drops of dew or spring rain. The overall forms are reminiscent of natural growth as it curves upward and out. An entire area is covered with small round beads that suggest budding but also to reflect light in this somewhat dark, monotone design. The beads in combination with stem, seeding and spider web stitches create textures that the all green scheme depends on for vitality. The criss-cross filling on the right is achieved with long straight stitches and tied down with tiny metallic ones. Kelly green metallic thread also contributes to the highlights of the design which is worked on a strong green, tightly woven linen. There are some accents in black, the only color outside of greens, added here.

Moving Forms

Varied forms that seem to be in movement are treated in different ways. Entirely covered with embroidered stitches, in largely taupe, tan, off-white to brown with accents of bright yellow and fuchsia; stem, chain, detached chain, laid work and spider web are used here. Some forms are left rather open while others are solidly filled and covered with stitches. The background fabric is natural linen and the frame is narrow, medium-finished wood.

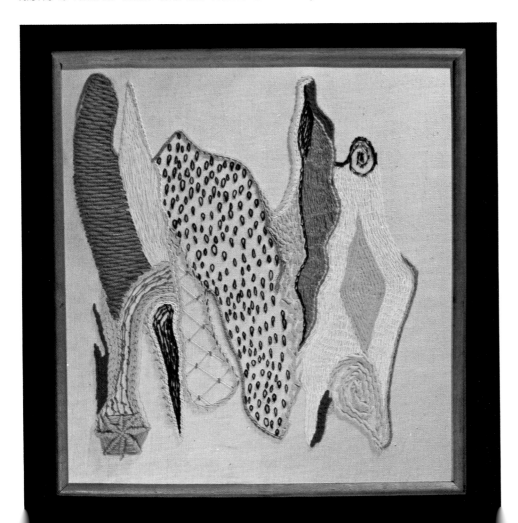

Shell Shock

The translucence of a certain shell is the theme here, so the design was carried out in delicate, cool colors and a variety of white and clear beads, some more lustrous than others. I wanted a lot of light reflection from the surface so I added pale blue metallic threads as accents here and there. To balance the pale blues, some dark blue was added in small amounts and repeated to pull the design together. Stem stitches and french knots are used against a white twill fabric that is tightly woven.

A Troll's Nosegay

The form at large is a very definite arrangement of massed flowers, expressive of some other place and time as they reflect the viewer who dares to get up close to smell their fragrance. Small silver glass beads are tacked on to throw off as much light reflection as possible. See page 87.

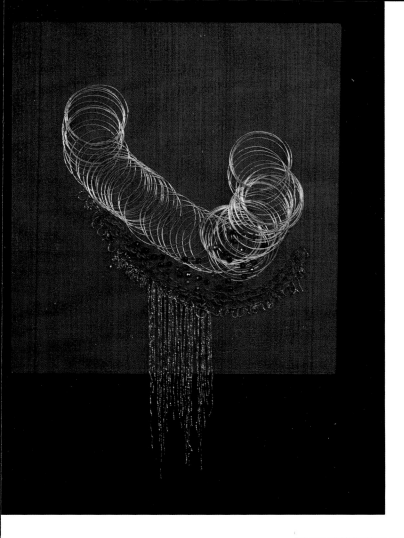

Cycling

Convolutions of brilliantly reflective copper wire are seen in close-up against Thai silk fabric. Most exciting are the many shapes and slices of shapes formed by the crossings of wire. The light is blinding at some points of the design, depending on the direction of the wire.

Aromatica

Abstraction of open bags of spices seen in tropical island markets is worked mostly in couching and stem stitches. The circular forms suggest the shape of the subject matter and variety is achieved through use of heavily textured threads, chenille, angora wool and metallics.

Mod Mum In the Round

An abstract chrysanthemum is conveyed through an arrangement of heavy dark green, shiny thread that outlines the desired form. The thread is couched with tiny straight stitches and all the emergent shapes resulting from the crossings of this thread become the major shapes of the design. These shapes are then filled with rhodes and eyelet stitches in brilliant colors; every green imaginable and a wide range of salmons, pinks, reds, fuchsias and purple. The colors are grouped according to their family with some merging. The design was worked on tan needlepoint canvas, size 16 mesh, in silk, wool, rayon, stranded and pearl cotton threads. There is a marvelous contrast in light reflection based on the contrasting properties of the threads. Texture adds further to the vitality of the design, both of canvas, thread and stitch.

The finished embroidery was stuffed in separate sections, following the shapes of the mum as they developed from the way the heavy thread crossed itself. The mum was then mounted softly, that is, taken off the stretcher (before stuffing) and stitched around its contour. It will be hung on the wall, as a sculpture, by means of a small ring which is attached to the backing fabric. See page 88 for close up.

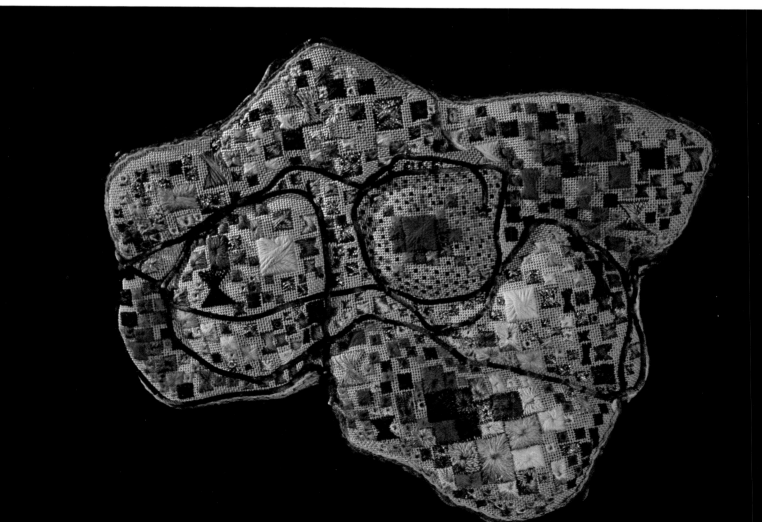

Renascence

Inspired by the poem of this name written by Edna St. Vincent Millay, this design reflects all the positive feelings that respond to renewal, growth, light and promise. Life and mood cycles correspond similarly, sad times, good times, ebbs and flows, cold of winter followed by warmth and promise of spring.

The design is stitched on needlepoint canvas in undulating lines of heavy handspun wool which had to be couched, rayon turkey work, chenille worked like fringe and straight stitches in zigzag design. The entire color scheme is green: pale, olive, blue-green, turquoise to dark green. Textures range from silky smooth to shaggy nubbly, all quite contrasting with the flat geometric canvas. The great feeling of movement in the composition is suggestive of renewal and surging growth. See page 39 for close up.

Bark Swatch

A study in texture, color and movement, this design grew out of the elementary knothole form and was worked in one stitch. The stem stitch conveys the graceful sway and swerve of the configurations and patterns in bark. Thick thin, smooth and shaggy threads of angora, wool, cotton and rayon project a tactile surface that bark suggests. The background is smooth, close weave white linen that remains in a secondary role to the design.

Perhaps you can take off from nature, in a direct fashion. Color, texture, shape, form are just outside the window. Birds in flight, the contour of an iris, patterns in the grass, a weeping cherry and further away, the galaxy, exotic foliage, shells, harvested wheat are just a few of the infinite number of embroiderable subjects. Just try to render the subject from eye to fabric as intuition guides you.

The cross section of a fruit or vegetable has been a good source of design. Notice the structure, texture, color, shape, size of seeds; select the essence and interpret it. Can you make a green pepper enchanting? Once again, I suggest keeping the embroidered version simple, free of too much minute detail. All art is selective and

Manhole cover
One of the visual images of our everyday life, this decorative manhole cover has an elaborate repeat pattern with cut-out holes. Observe the many images surrounding you and borrow what you choose for the shaping of your own creative vision.

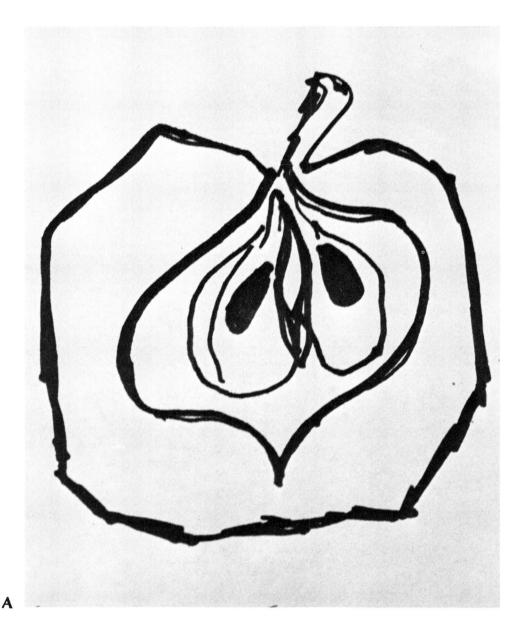

A

Apple cross section

The apple is stitched in shades of rust, salmon, taupe and some greens. The shape is quite close to realism with interpretations that are personal. For example, I appliquéd pieces of printed fabric to suggest seeds in the center and three oval-shaped leather shapes bottom right. Open, lacy stitches are woven over the left area of the apple; chain, outline and buttonhole stitches complete the scheme. Notice how the worked-out design changes from the original sketch, but preserves the basic form. This is what happens eighty-five per cent of the time, as you really are faced with the shaping of the design.

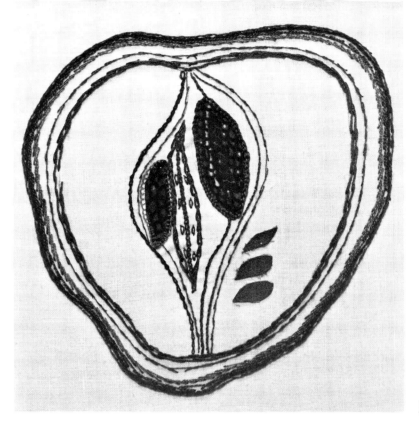

B

C

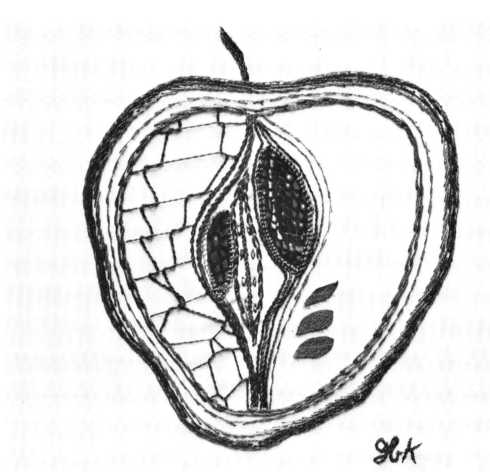

Jitters

An embroidered design can evoke states of mind as well as any medium. This is quite evident in the zigzag, jagged, thick and thin lines of straight stitches that are so suggestive of tension and restlessness. The small exercise is another example of simple self expression and a way of approaching the making of design. The colors I chose had to express the mood so they are black, red and fuchsia, all vigorous, bold and restless.

your impression of the subject is a valid beginning. Picasso glorified many a lemon in inventive ways so no theme is too humble.

Every day scenes in our environmental landscape are inviting to design. A street scene of trash cans and debris, a manhole cover, railroad ties, a stack of firewood, a bridge, a sidewalk market, sailboats, the pattern of cobblestones on an old square.

The inner landscape is especially provocative, leaving you more on your own to conjure up images and ways to project the jitters, grief, anxiety, fantasy, joy, a nightmare.

The artists Klee and Miro focused on the playful mood in art and used fanciful images to express it. The viewer is free to interpret

Wood pile
Handsome pattern of stacked wood opens many doors to design if you consider the textures, light and dark tones, linear marks in the wood, angles and shapes present. Even the black spaces between logs are positive shapes for designing.

from his own frame of reference which gives the experience many levels of enjoyment.

Current events and social issues, ecology, racial discord, war are all subject to the concern and scrutiny of the artist. Literature, a musical phrase, your favorite poem, a myth, biblical subjects can all inspire ideas for design. Imagine portraying Pandora's box with all manner of symbols and images spilling out! In the last two months, I have seen four versions of Joseph's coat.

Paintings, calligraphy, sculpture, graphic and advertising art are still other sources of design but I urge you not to resort to copying other art. Interpret, use a part of a work to enlarge upon it and expand it into something original. Copying reduces art to craft and in the end takes away the joy of discovery and original statement. The result should be a sort of variation on a theme, some borrowing, enriched by your own feelings and ideas. There are no charts of the designs in this book. Indeed, the work defies the limitations and boundaries of step by step "how to do it". The work is free, somewhat experimental and almost always evolved in a gradual growth, building one idea upon another in a subjective way. It is so personal that it tells its own story and my trains of thought.

Hopefully when you have reached the end, you will find you are at the beginning of an odyssey into an art form that invites invention and exploration and is off to new directions beyond stamped linen, painted canvas, embroidery kits and charted designs.

2

Stitches

Stitchery can be worked on anything that will permit the passing of a needle, from tightly woven flannel to fiber glass curtain mesh. The more orthodox and usual materials are evenly woven needlepoint canvas with holes that act as guides to counted stitches or linens and cottons that allow more freely arranged stitches that ignore the weave of background materials. While needlepoint stitches are dependent on the weave of the canvas, they can be adapted to other types of fabric in combination with more free wheeling stitches and vice versa. Almost any stitch can ignore the weave of the background fabric and indeed, a more interesting and vital work can result from this blending. Stitches are a tool and should be exploited and approached with abandon rather than obedience. The stitches used in this book are illustrated on Aida cotton, a fabric that is both loosely and tightly woven so that counted as well as free stitches can be visualized together, using and ignoring the weave of the cloth. Here and there a stitch will be shown on needlepoint canvas because it really works best there and because I want to point up the visual differences of stitches while making the point that they can be combined and interchanged most of the time. The tent stitch is a needlepoint stitch that really does not adapt to tightly woven fabric and belongs best on needlepoint canvas. The basics of stitch making are illustrated

Flora

Hint of flower form has sheer voile petals which are veined with stem stitches and accented with tiny, white, opaque beads. The petals are appliquéd on a patterned all-wool background fabric of upholstery weight to emphasize the contrast between materials. The center of the flower is heavily embroidered, almost encrusted with French knots, spider webs and seeding in brown, tans, metallic brown, and white.

because they are the starting point of invention. Some variations are added near by, often in the context of design, that is, outlining a form, filling a shape and setting up a direction. I couldn't possibly chart the unlimited and marvelous changes and irregularities of which a stitch is capable but the idea is revealed in the designs that follow. I tend to de-emphasize the actual stitch in favor of what effects it produces, how it integrates into the design, teams up with other stitches and more of its own kind. One stitch, imaginatively used, will have more impact than a one-work exhibit of all you know. My choice of stitches here relates to what they would do for the design. They are the best known stitches. As the book is not meant to be a glossary of embroidery stitches, there is a limited selection. Delve further as you wish to add to your storehouse of stitches or invent new ones.

Stitches create dynamic lines and shapes, outline forms, suggest movement and produce texture, spread color, establish direction.

Dancers
Swirling lines that overlap and cross suggest the movements of classical dance. The gold silk and metallic threads convey the richness of costume and set generally part of the staging. The cluster of gold metal faceted beads is meant to represent the corps de ballet, waiting perhaps to make their entrance. The design is embroidered on earth brown velveteen in one stitch throughout, the stem stitch.

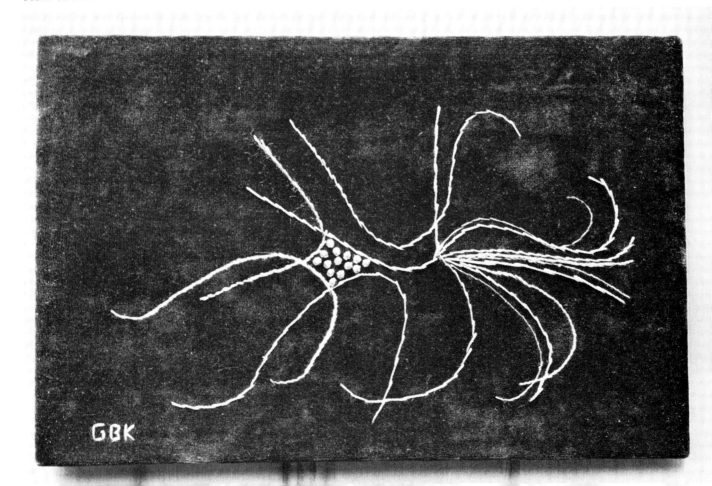

Each has its own flavor, a character that sets it apart from the others. Some stitches are square, some raised and rough, some open, some closed and tight, some linear and smooth. There are single stitches like the straight stitch and composites like the smyrna and eyelet. Stitches are straight, looped, knotted, crossed and woven. Worked alone or in a row, a stitch is quite different than worked closely together with others. Massed in a large area, stitches lose their individuality and merge with the rest to project a bold impact. Spaced wide apart, stitches are lacy and convey a

Stria

Earlier version of Stria indicates growth as well as subtraction. Compare the final version with this and notice that I ripped off the heavy ravelled rope at the bottom, which did not seem to complete the design properly. Beads and other details were added later.

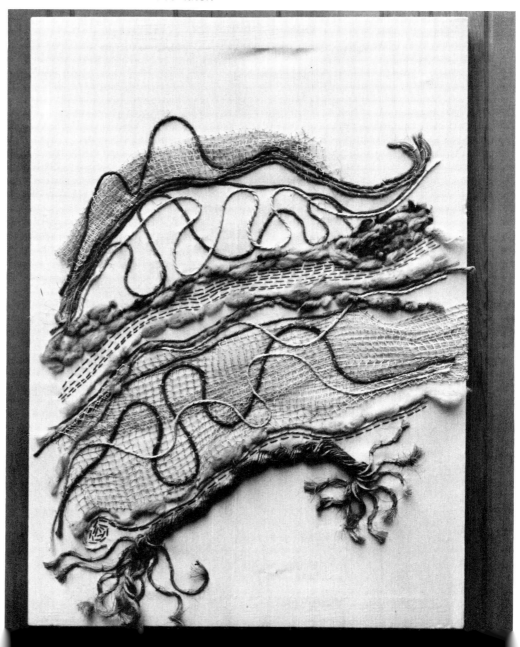

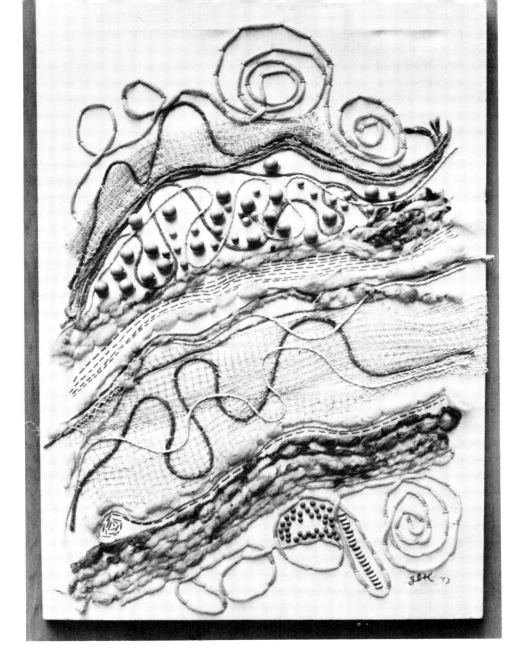

Stria

Cord, twine, rug yarn and handspun, hand-dyed wool are couched on a shiny rayon fabric in linear patterns in a monochromatic color scheme. Netting is appliquéd to add to the textural study experienced in a woods walk when foliage and paths are encountered in brush-like abundance. Large and small wooden beads in natural color represent all the woods rubble, gravel, sand, stones, pebbles, etc. . . . There are highs and lows in the design as well as contrasts in character of materials: hairy, smooth, solid, see-through, sheen and matte.

more spotty and fragmented spread of effects. With every change of stitch there is a change of texture. A long straight stitch results in a smoothly textured surface that almost looks quilted. Smooth, long stitches pick up light and where they change direction, the light reflects unevenly in enchanting ways. Rough, nubby stitches worked together with smooth ones make for a polarity that enlivens the design. Be a bit wary of patterned and pile fabrics which tend to hide stitches. A tiny delicate stitch worked in fine thread on velveteen will sink and disappear in the nap of the fabric. To offset this, use a heavier thread, loosen up on stitch tension, or couch the finer threads to get a visible effect from your stitch. Stitches worked on plaid or checked fabric must be boldly scaled to make any creative impression, let alone be seen. Decide for yourself which stitches best create the excitement, the accents, highlights and design effects you want. Learn the basics, then depart from the numbered "ins and outs" of needle and thread. If you change the position of the needle, the stitch will be changed. Alter its angle, length, width, spacing, tension and direction and there is instant variation. Work stitches on a scrap of fabric in swirling lines and tight geometric patterns. Explore them in different weights of thread and in light and dark colors. Notice how changed a stitch is when worked with a heavy thread after a fine one! Start outlining a shape with one stitch and change it part way around to enliven the contour. Work a stitch on top of another and interlace lines of stitches to see what effects result. Working these stitch exercises and testing their potential will broaden and deepen your virtuosity. It will also give you the necessary confidence to design more freely yet in control of all the intriguing effects possible to inventive work. Don't be too concerned with names, labels and categories. Some stitches are known by several names, which has nothing to do with their look or function. Use them as you wish, where you wish, blending, distorting and experimenting. Be an impeccable craftsman, securing all threads on the back of your work and watching stitch tension to avoid pulled, strained looking embroidery. Clip all secured threads closely so that the underside of your work is as neat and tidy as the front. To start embroidering, I usually leave a two-inch end of thread on the

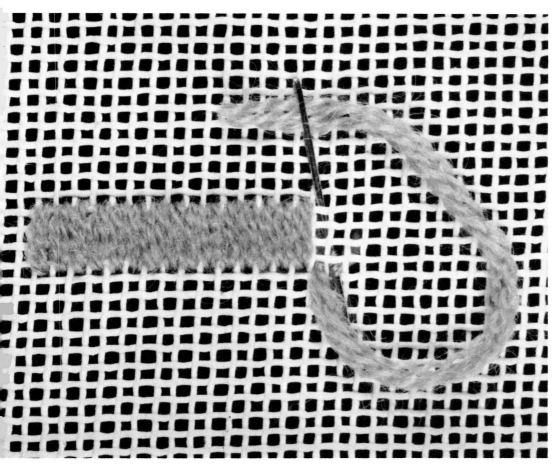

Straight stitches

A row of straight stitches evenly worked over four threads of needlepoint canvas in persian wool. On STRAIGHT OP (p. 103), the entire design was worked in even rows of this stitch in black and white.

back which I later weave through finished stitches to secure it. Usually I avoid starting with knots . . . but here and there it may be necessary and harmless.

Most stitches evolve from the straight stitch, which is known variously as the satin, gobelin and florentine stitch. It can be long, short, upright, tilted, knotted, looped, lined up in even rows, scattered randomly, crossed and zig-zagged. The straight stitch adapts to a wide range of fabrics and can be worked in rigid or free wheeling design arrangements.

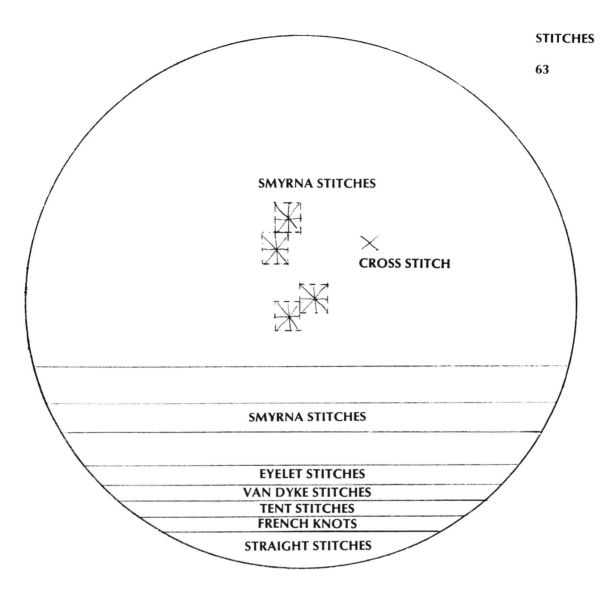

SMYRNA STITCHES

CROSS STITCH

SMYRNA STITCHES

EYELET STITCHES

VAN DYKE STITCHES

TENT STITCHES

FRENCH KNOTS

STRAIGHT STITCHES

Detail of Sunburst #2
This photo and diagram emphasize the variety of stitches that can be used together compatibly. Both photo and diagram are turned side ways compared to photo in color section. The stitches can be used any way at all.

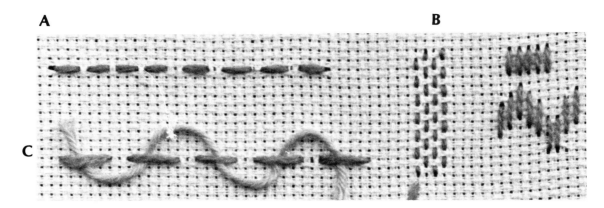

Running stitch

(A.) Straight stitches of the same or uneven length are worked in and out of the fabric. The spacing is optional, depending on the effect desired. Masses of running stitches. **(B.)** fill a design shape quite rapidly. To vary the running stitch, thread through each one with a contrasting yarn **(C.)** without picking up any background fabric. A blunt tip needle sliding under will link up the stitches in a dramatic way.

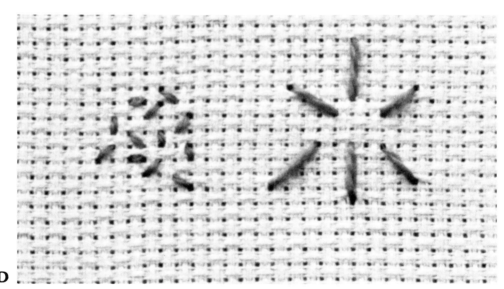

Seeding

(D.) Tiny straight stitches tilted in every which way will resemble falling snow. Different colors and/or thread can be combined in an area of seeding to provide a backdrop for design or to unify a series of motifs. Vary the stitch simply by allowing it to be loose on the surface, in short, do not pull it all the way, leaving a tiny loop. You can also work two seed stitches together as a unit for a stronger design motif.

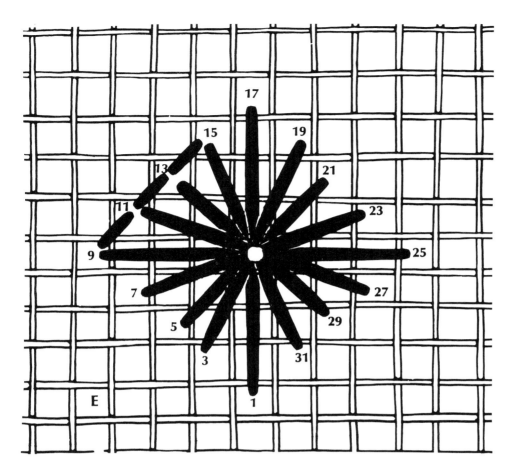

Diamond Eyelet

(E.) This is a composite stitch made up of 16 tilted and straight stitches that radiate out of the same center. Each stitch goes back through the center mesh again and again. The stitches forming the points of the diamond are worked over four threads, those in between over three, then two, then three and the point over four again. The outside edge forms a diamond. On fabrics other than needlepoint canvas, the stitch can be worked unevenly while still getting the shape of the diamond.

Eyelet

(F.) For variation, square the outside edge by making all the stitches the same length. Because you go into the center mesh so many times, do not start with a knot which will get in the way. Leave a tail of thread that can later be woven through the back of finished stitches.

E

F

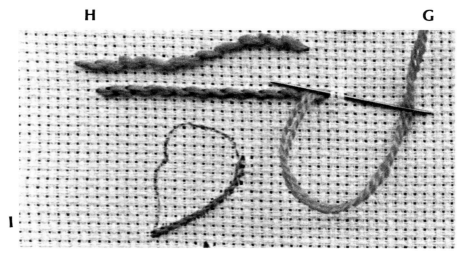

Stem stitch

(G.) This versatile, linear stitch is especially useful in establishing contours of shapes and forms, filling design areas and suggesting direction and movement. It can be worked with varying thicknesses of thread. It is shown creating a straight line, **(H.)** a slight curve and **(I.)** outlining a leaf. Bring the needle out at 1, insert it at 2, back out to the last stitch made at 3, which is the same hole with 1, insert at 4, go back to last stitch made which is the same hole as 2. Continue from here in the same way, working rows from left to right. You create a circle by working the stem stitch in a counter clockwise direction and turning your work as you go. Always control the thread with your left thumb so that it hangs below the needle.

Couching

(J.) This is a form of appliqué using threads rather than fabric. It consists of tying down at intervals one or more threads by another, either the same type and color or contrasting thread and color. Usually the thread is too bulky or nubby to be drawn through the background fabric. The simplest way to attach a thread is with small straight stitches but other stitches will couch more dramatically: french knots, buttonhole, cross, herringbone and chain stitches. Unusual threads will also enhance a couched line: shiny rayon for wool, silk for metallic, for example. Smoothly linear effects can be achieved with couching and whole areas of design can be filled threads that are couched against the fabric. Several threads can be couched together and parted at intervals to be tied separately. A couched line can be arranged in any shape, **(K.)** geometric or free form. A grid-like design **(L.)** can be worked of couched threads and used as a see-through filling or just because it is an interesting form. Just criss-cross long straight stitches and tie the inter-sections of threads with tiny stitches.

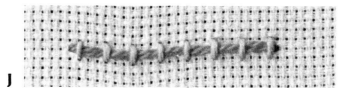

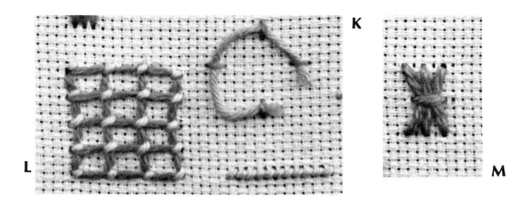

L

Sheaf stitch

(M.) Work three or four upright straight stitches of even or erratic length and tie them across the middle with a small horizontal straight stitch. A thick thread will produce a bulky raised stitch and the shape of an hour glass if the stitch around the middle is drawn tightly.

Four sided stitch

(N.) Four straight stitches, two vertical and two horizontal are worked to form a square. The outside square is shown here over seven threads of fabric. The next square is then worked inside it over five threads, then over three, and finally in the center, over one. Change the threads and colors to enliven the square or use graded shades to achieve a glow of color. This stitch performs best on even weave fabric.

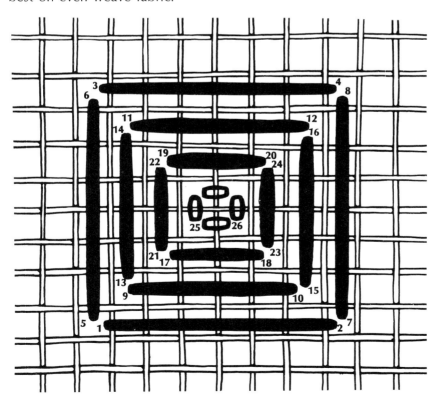

N

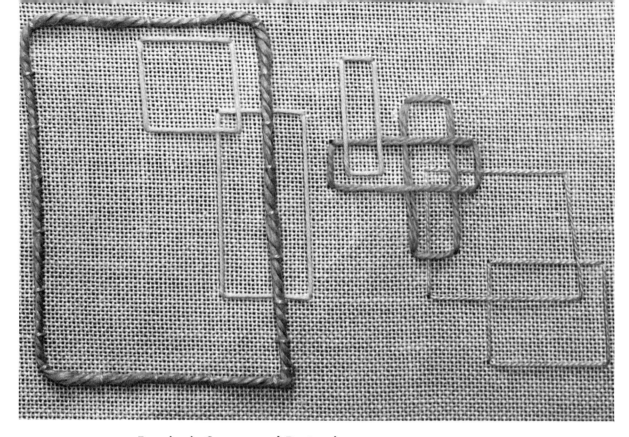

Exercise in Squares and Rectangles

Elementary geometric shapes overlap in varying arrangements with heavy and fine threads using straight stitches and couching on open linen. In one version, black plastic bugle-type beads are strewn over the design to test ability to add a worthy dimension. One can improve upon this lay-out by manipulating as desired. When and if satisfied, stitch in place.

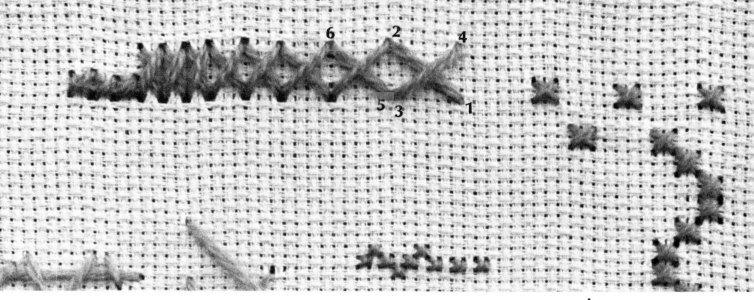

Cross stitch

(A.) Straight stitches cross over one another in a variety of ways and one or more times. The cross stitch is the result of one tilted stitch crossing over another stitch tilted in the opposite direction. When worked in even rows all top crosses should slant in the same direction and each cross should be completed before going on. In freer design, cross them any way you wish; space and scale them in a variety of ways and work them in different directions, diagonally, vertically, horizontally as set up on the Aida cloth.

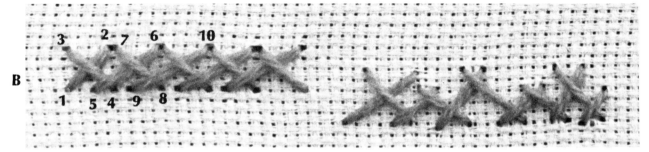

Herringbone stitch

(B.) Herringbone is marvelously versatile and capable of different effects dependent on spacing which can cause it to be squatty, solid or lacy and seethrough. As with all stitches, the weight and character of thread will affect the look of the stitch. Usually worked in rows from left to right, bring needle up at 1, insert at 2, up at 3 (going back a tiny space) insert at 4, and back up at 5. Continue in this fashion as far as you work. Rows of herringbone stitches, overlapped and interlaced, create marvelous color blendings: luminescence, glowing and shading. Worked very close, the stitch will cover a leaf shape thoroughly. **(C.)** It also couches a heavy thread very effectively. **(D.)**

Smyrna stitch

(E.) This square, raised mound is simply a basic cross stitch with an upright cross over it. A needlepoint stitch, usually worked over from two to four threads of canvas, it can be worked with planned irregularity on differently woven background fabrics. When it is tiny, it emerges a tight bump and when large, it appears a bold, textured mound in the design. Thicker thread is needed if the stitch is enlarged to be certain that is covers the fabric thoroughly.

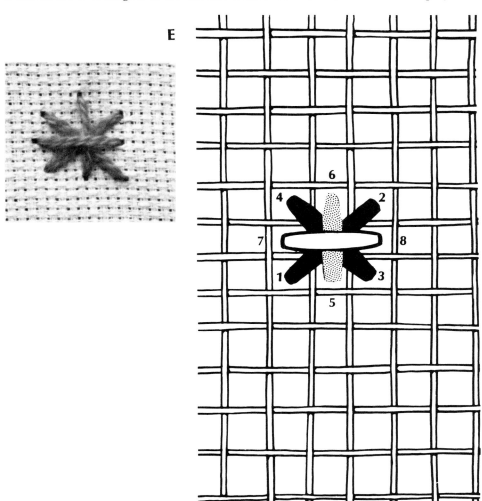

Smyrna stitch on needlepoint canvas

Three stages of the working of a smyrna stitch left to right, starting with a cross stitch and worked over four threads of canvas; a straight row of completed smyrna stitches and a row of diagonal smyrna stitches.

Exercises in Smyrna Stitches
Two versions of a simple arrangement of Smyrna stitches show how different
the design will be when materials are changed. In one instance, large round
plastic discs are interspersed with the stitches, their white surface brightening

the design surface. In the other, dark round beads are used as accents but they do little for the scheme. The three stitches at the top of the photograph show the working of the stitch.

F

Rhodes stitch

(**F.**) Another especially high-rise stitch, the Rhodes stitch crosses over and over itself and adapts best to canvas and looser weaves. On the Aida cloth, it is worked over a total of twenty-eight threads, beginning with a long tilted stitch, from lower left to upper right, over seven intersections of fabric threads. On needlepoint canvas, the stitch is worked over twenty-four threads and is shown in three stages of development: the first long tilted stitch, halfway when it looks like an hour glass and the finished raised square. It can be made over any number of threads, no less than three, the result is intriguing tactile character. The halfway point of the stitch is a handsome design form that can be considered a variation.

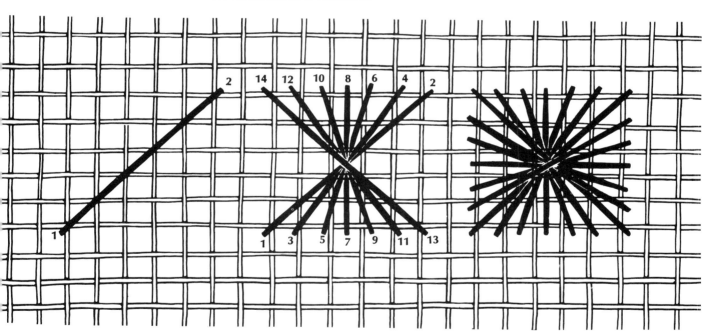

Van Dyke stitch

(G.) This is a linear, high-rise stitch that begins with a cross stitch and is worked from the top down. Bring the needle out at 1, insert at 2, come out at 3, insert at 4, out again at 5, just under 1. Now slide a blunt tip needle from right to left under the crossed threads made by 1 and 2, 3 and 4 without picking up any of the material, and reinsert the needle at 6, just under 4. Bring the needle out again at 7 and slide it as before, from right to left under the last crossed threads, gently pulling thread up as a small braid forms. The thicker the thread used, the more bold and dramatic the braid. The van dyke is incomparable in establishing a strong textured, curved or straight line in design and it adapts to all fabrics equally well. See Detail of SUNBURST #2 (p. 62).

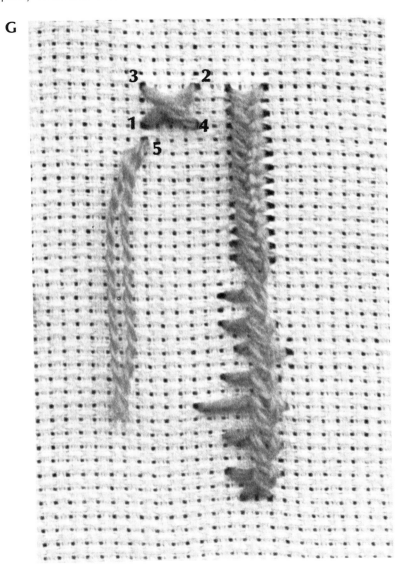

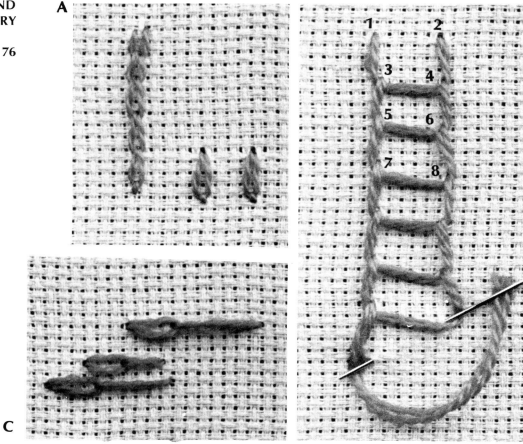

Looped stitches
Chain Stitch

A looped stitch is formed by curving a straight stitch, holding it down with the left thumb and pulling the thread through the loop that has formed. (**A.**) A chain stitch is basically a closed loop with the thread looped under the needle so that it can be pulled through it. I work it from the top down and if necessary, the work can be turned to facilitate this.

Bring the needle out at 1, holding the thread down below the needle to form a loop, insert at 2 just next to 1 and out at 3 just inside the loop, still controlling the thread. For the next chain, go back into completed link at 4 and continue. End a line by taking a small straight tack down stitch over the last loop. (**B.**) Vary the chains by making large and small, open and closed chains with different types of threads. Watch stitch tension to avoid puckers.

An interesting way to fill a space is to work detached chain stitches (**C.**) in an allover pattern; this is simply a single link of the chain, tacked down with a short or long stitch.

(D.) Open the single link at the top, tack it down to fasten it and you have the fly stitch, still another variation of the chain stitch. Masses of fly stitches can be scattered behind design motifs to unify them and provide a filling for the space.

(E.) Rows of chains can be zigzagged and the chain itself can be made wide and square. Secure the square chain with two tiny tack-down stitches in the last two corners. **(F.)** A narrow chain can be worked right over the wide, square one. Use these examples of variations as your starting point to further invention with this maneuverable stitch.

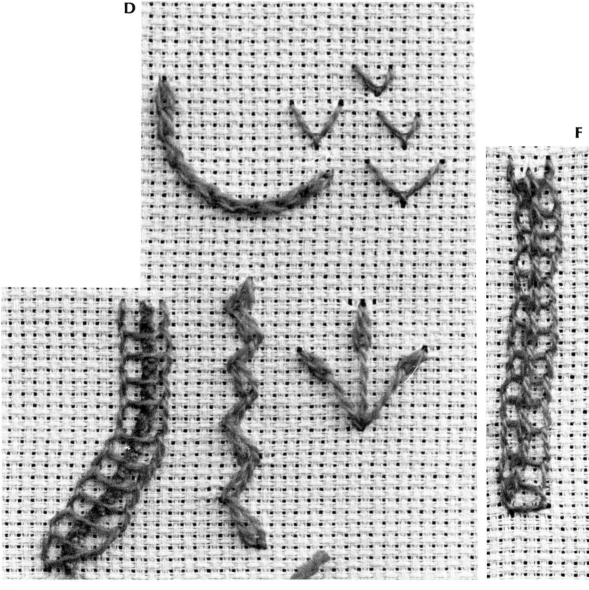

D

F

E

Buttonhole stitch

(G.) This stitch is worked from left to right, bring the needle out at 1. Holding the thread with the left thumb to form a loop and with the needle pointing toward you, insert at 2, coming out again at 3 and continuing in this way. Variations occur when the length and spacing of the stitches are changed along the line which can of course be straight, (H.) wavy or scalloped. Buttonhole can be worked in a perfect circle, (I.) in an open or very close placement of stitches. See HOMAGE TO CIRCLES (p. 21).

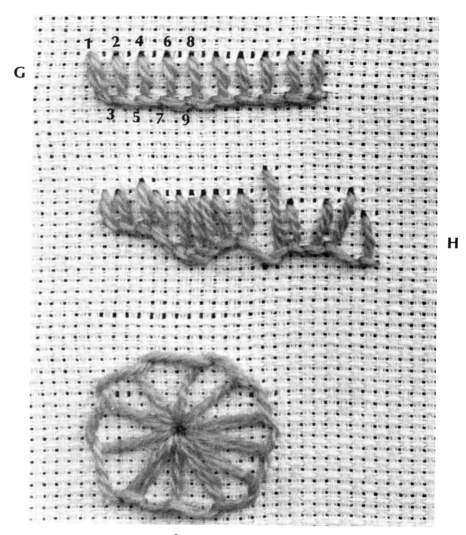

J

Turkey work or Rya stitch

(J.) Work this stitch in horizontal rows no matter what shape is to be filled. I find it easier to stitch from the bottom up so that the finished row is behind and the loops that form do not get in the way. The needle is inserted in the front of the fabric at 1. and is brought out at 2, leaving an end of thread loose on the front. Moving from left to right with thread below the needle on a line with 1. and 2., insert at 3. and come up next to or in the same hole with 1. Draw the thread tight, holding on to the loose end to keep it from going into the fabric or to the underside. With the thread above the needle, insert the needle at 4, come up at 3. keeping looped thread under control with your left thumb. Now with thread once again below the needle, insert at 5. and pull up tight. Continue in this way, alternating the position of the thread, leaving a loop below then above the needle and pulling it tight. To achieve a thick pile, make short stitches and work the rows very close together. When the area or shape is filled, cut the loops. It may be that you will leave uncut loops or a mix of both for a desired effect. To get a shaggy look, make long and short loops; cut some and leave a few uncut. Combine different threads in the needle for further excitement in color and texture of your pile or fringe. See TYPEWRITER RIBBON, SUNBURST # 3, MAUVE MAJESTY.

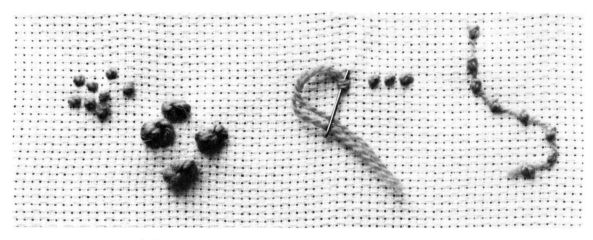

French knot

(A.) This is a rough, raised, rounded bump that can be worked in neat, even rows, on top of existing stitches or scattered around like petals in a wind.
(B.) It will also couch a thread most decoratively. Bring the needle out at 1, holding it horizontally against the fabric. Wrap it once with the thread held taut by the left thumb. Revolve the needle clockwise just next to the point from which it emerged, at down and pull through to the back, keeping the thread taut until the knot is drawn tight. For thicker knots, use thicker thread. A large form can be packed full of closely worked french knots for a pebbled surface effect.

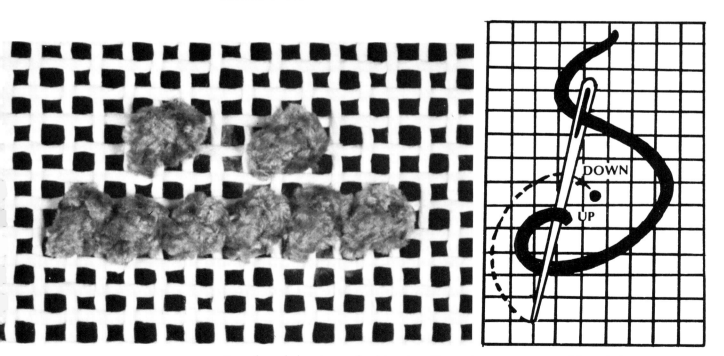

Two french knots worked in chenille and an even row of french knots.

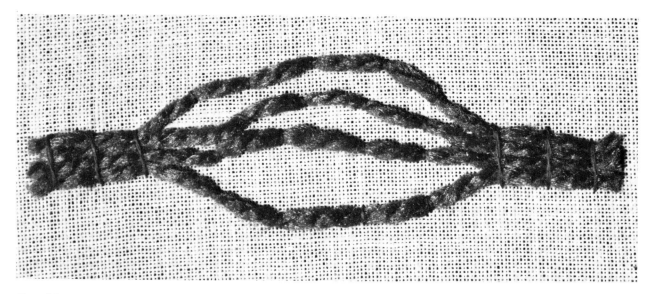

Couching

Four heavy threads couched close together then separated in an open pattern.

One heavy thread is couched here with contrasting thread in herringbone stitch. The background fabric is a rather open linen.

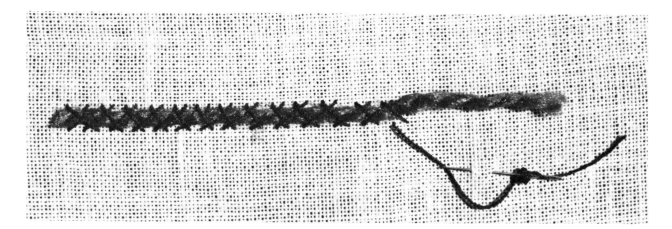

C

Whipped Spider web stitch

(**C.**) Work 8 radiating straight stitches, evenly spaced like the spokes of a wheel. Working clockwise, round and round, take back stitches over the spokes until they are thoroughly covered. Use a blunt tip needle and do not pick up any fabric; slide under each spoke. A large spider requires more spokes. For variation, leave some spokes uncovered and deliberately keep the spokes uneven in length and spacing.

Woven Spider web stitch

(**D.**) Start by working an odd number of spokes, by adding an extra half stitch to the circle. Bring the needle out at the center and work round and round, sliding the needle over and under the spokes alternately, until they are filled with thread. (under 1, over two, under 3, over 4.) Color can be changed any-where along the way as can the type of thread so that the center may be one color, the outer circle another. (**E.**) Spokes can be laid down without meeting in the center or they can be placed side by side (**F.**) or fan-shaped, then whipped or woven over, according to my exercise.

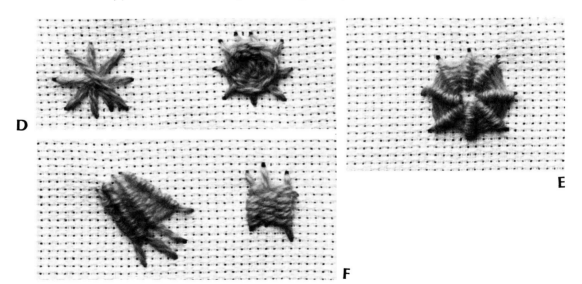

D

E

F

Zigzag straight stitches

Two rows of straight stitches, the length of four canvas threads, step up and down the canvas in zigzag pattern. The stitches on row two share a mesh with those on row one. I combined this pattern with spider webs, tent stitch and french knots in SUN BURST #2, page 62.

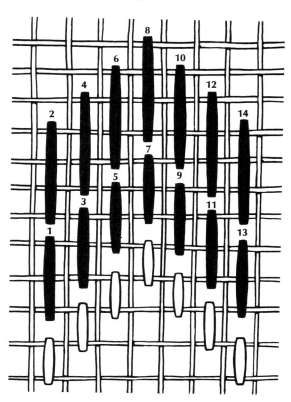

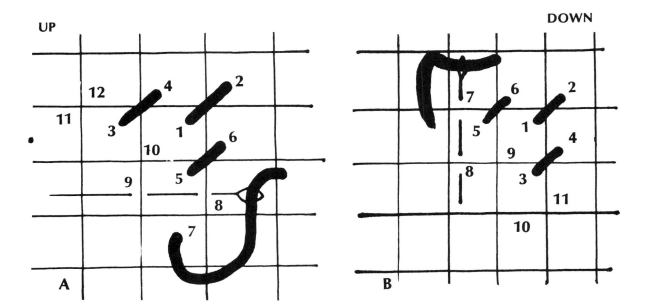

UP

DOWN

A

B

Basket weave stitch

The tent stitch can be worked on needlepoint canvas in diagonal rows starting in the upper right corner where you make one stitch, then another, one mesh left of and on the same row with it. (stitch 1 and 2 in diagrams) Stitches 3 and 4 are worked next. Notice that the corner has been set up. Next work stitches 5 and 6, observing the tiny triangle beginning to take shape. Continue making diagonal rows from upper left to lower right alternately and do not turn the canvas.

The first stitch of an up row is worked directly under the last stitch of the last row and the needle is held horizontally. The first stitch of a down row is worked on the same row but one mesh left of the last stitch made. The needle is held vertically on down rows. A basket weave pattern forms on the underside of the stitchery, giving this method the name, basket weave stitch. All tent stitches look alike on the top side, regardless of method. From row to row, there is a neat dovetailing between stitches.

B

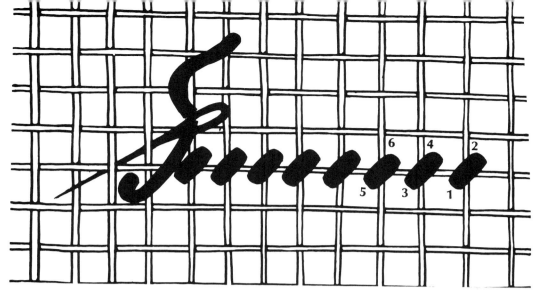

The continental stitch

The tent stitch is worked from lower left to upper right over the intersection of one warp and one weft thread of needlepoint canvas. It does not adapt well to other fabrics because it depends on the evenly spaced, open meshes or holes of the canvas which is sized to give it body and hold the stitches in place. Tent stitches make good gap fillers between large stitches.

The continental method of working the tent stitch is pictured here in horizontal rows, worked from right to left. At the end of a row, turn the work upside down and stitch back. The direction will still be right to left. The continental stitch can be worked vertically, from the top down. All individual stitches should slant in the same direction.

Chain stitch exercise
Rows of chain stitches reflect an abstract idea of people lined up, waiting for a bus. It is a simple exercise as well as my personal vision of a well-known, often experienced scene. It reveals how distortable the chain stitch is and how able it is to convey images of design. This exercise is a perfect example of how you can explore any stitch, letting the stitch itself be the design form.

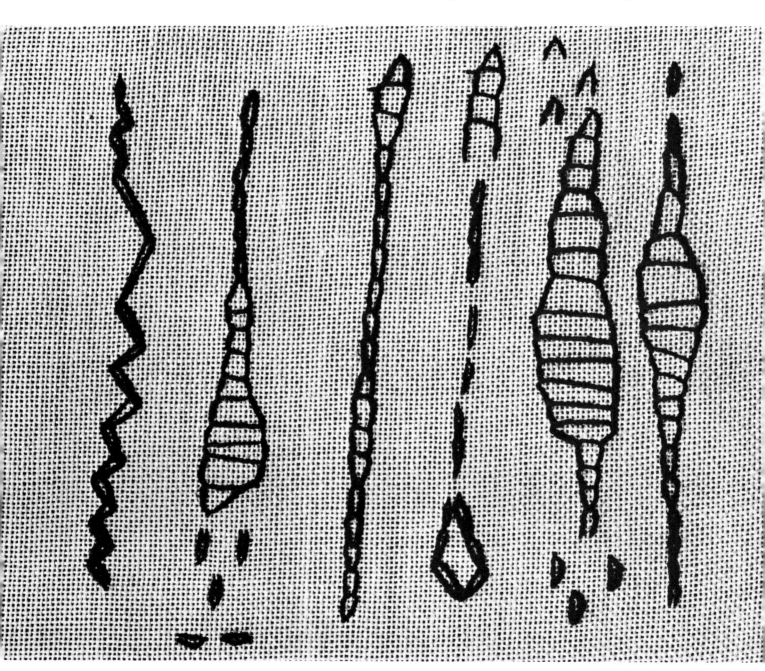

Scribbled chains
You don't have to be Da Vinci to explore with pen the many ways of working chain or other stitches. Here on paper are narrow, wide, circular, open, detached and zigzag chains, very casually scribbled.

Detail of Mod Mum

Close-up view of the center of the design reveals square shapes contrasting with the curved, couched, shiny, heavy thread that is so important in this composition. Small, large, shiny, dull stitches are visible against the nice texture of exposed needlepoint canvas. Tonal variation shows up here as well as flat stitches with bumpy ones. Notice how the heavy curved thread is attached to the canvas with widely spaced small straight stitches. Rhodes stitches of all sizes dominate the center of the design. Note hourglass image at the upper right which is the half way mark of the Rhodes stitch. See color section.

3

Color

"But we almost never . . . see a single color unconnected and unrelated to other colors. Colors present themselves in continuing flux, constantly related to changing neighbors and changing conditions."*

Color, the first impression communicated in design, is seldom what it seems. It is the most relative part of art. Remote mountains appear to be mauve or soft blue when in reality they are barren rocks or covered with foliage. Two people munching apples will disagree on what red they are. Color, shape, and texture are made visible through light. Color is one thing when bleached by sunlight and quite another at nightfall by artificial light. Yellows tend to evaporate, blues deepen and reds look brownish. Texture will modify these effects; the shiny surfaces will reflect light while the opaque ones will deepen as they absorb light. Color choices should be made by natural light but weighed in both settings, especially if the design is to be seen in a dark hall.

Color is affected by adjacent colors. Surround a bright yellow with darker and lighter shades of yellow and see the changes in it, side by side with different shades. Try the same yellow with red, green, or cornflower blue; there are still other changes in the yellow. Against a black background, color is bolder and more dazzling. Against white it seems deeper, as there is so much in-

* *Interaction of Color*, Joseph Albers, Yale University Press, New Haven, 1963.   **89**

tense light in white that it overpowers other colors. Black and white used to outline other colors will isolate and bring them out.

My approach to color choice is intuitive and rather emotional, certainly not academic. If I respond to it positively, I use it. If it contributes nothing or diminishes the scheme, I discard the color. It must enhance the design, bring subtlety, drama, animation and sometimes dissonance.

Color conveys the emotion of design as well as the vitality, energy or subtlety desired. The excitement of using color is in the blending, accenting, clashing and dazzling effects possible. Go beyond the rules, canons, vogues and taboos; choose and use colors exuberantly.

Hue is the family to which a color belongs. Value is its lightness and darkness. Red, blue, and yellow are called primaries because all others derive from them. Red and yellow produce orange, purple comes from the mixing of red and blue, and green is the offspring of blue and yellow.

Red is considered a warm, animated color that imparts vigor and advances before the eye. As bright red mixes with blue, it tends to become a cooler, quieter red. Blues, greens and grays are cool, low-keyed colors, restful and receding from the eye. Lighter, paler colors evoke delicacy; deeper ones convey stronger impressions.

Feelings and moods are expressed through color, melancholy through blue, aggression through red, dignity through purple, well-being through yellow. There are symbolic ideas suggested by color. Green is favored because it symbolizes growth and renewal. White is associated with purity and black with grief and, in couture, chic. Color may go in and out of fashion cyclically; what is in today is out next season and may have been unthinkable in the past. Be your own style setter and choose what your feelings and instincts dictate. Once again, nature is the best source of marvelous color blending; even when seemingly dissonant, colors are compatible and vital. Notice the spectrum of autumn colors: muddy greens, pale and black greens, gold, lemon, mustard, bright yellow, russet, bittersweet, turkey red, mulberry, garnet and magenta. The nuances of summer, the iridescence of a peacock's feather, a field of tulips, the colors in a grotto are a few sources of color inspiration, not to be literally copied, however. Translate and interpret nature without feeling restricted by her.

". . . a tree trunk could be vermilion, a sky could be solid orange, a face could be divided down its middle by a green line with constrasting colors on either side, as part of a color structure owing no allegiance to the actual color of trees, skies or faces but existing as an independent abstraction."*

Think of color as a means of getting across your personal emotion and vision.

In embroidery, overlap threads to mix and build layers of color. To get solid areas of color, intertwine and superimpose stitches. Work them close together. Lay transparent fabrics over one another to change color and introduce tonal nuances. An interesting experiment is to dip a completed stitchery made of many different threads and still on its stretcher frame, into a pot of dye. Each thread will absorb the dye in varying amounts and ways. A monochrome color scheme of all sorts of shades will result. The different textures of the threads and the varying reflections of light on their surfaces affect the color so that some will glisten, some will be low key, some will be bright, some flat.

Color and texture are inseparable in embroidery; they are so interdependent. A very textured stitch like the french knot will appear darker. Conversely a light-colored thread will reveal the texture more decidedly. The same texture in a black yarn may not show up at all. Luminosity and iridescence are achieved by working five to seven closely graded shades of one color side by side. Interesting vibrations result from using two different colors through the eye of the same needle, purple with hot pink, for example. Black and white, used exactly this way, will produce a tweeded surface. An interesting way of introducing color to the surface is through holes cut in the background fabric which are backed with other colors. It is important to keep the background fabric and color of the threads in tune. Neutral fabrics are amenable to a glorious array of colors while colored and busy backgrounds may set up limitations with which you must cope. In the decision stage, move colors around the fabric, observing all interactions. To em-

* *Mainstreams of Modern Art*, John Canaday, Simon and Schuster, New York, 1959.

phasize the depth of one color, place a lighter one next to it. Each color used will affect the others, either bringing them out or subduing, sometimes adding just the right ingredient to a scheme. Once choices are firm, introduce repeats and accents throughout the design. Repetition of color as well as other elements of design is the rhythm that animates and unifies it. Toss in an occasional unexpected in controlled amounts, and above all, get color to work for you in a spontaneous way. Exploit it with daring and with verve.

It is capable of glowing, warming, cooling, quieting, luring, dazzling and gyrating.

4

Textures

"We touch things to assure ourselves of reality. We touch the objects we love. We touch the things we form . . ."*

Texture appeals to the eye as well as the touch. It is a way of seeing with your fingers the surface of the materials and objects around you. The tactile quality of these things can be lustrous, matte, shaggy, smooth, stippled, downy, etc. Light heightens texture in the sense that it makes it more visible. Flat, smooth fabric, like satin, will catch the light and reflect it. Opaque fabrics, like velveteen and flannel, will absorb light so that there is no reflection. Run your fingers over the materials that attract you visually, to get the feel of their surface character. A busily textured fabric will limit the added design. It would be better to work on a subdued, plain background fabric to allow stitches to have top billing. Any textile that will not be covered completely with stitches should be interesting and a worthy background to design. As the background becomes busier and bolder, the stitches and threads must grow in scale. Stitches have their tactile differences. Masses of french knots are nubby and rough like gravel on a path. Worked directly next to long, smooth upright stitches, there is a dramatic contrast in tactile effect. Contrasts are most effective when varied

* On Weaving, Anni Albers, Wesleyan University Press, Middleton, Connecticut, 1965.

93

Top: Two rows turkey work, cut loops in combination with a row of straight stitches in between. Left column: opaque glass bead, hardware washer, plastic hardware ring. Right: iridescent paillette applied to tent stitches, French knots, vertical row of van dyke stitch. Two Rhodes stitches worked halfway and backed by tent stitches

textures are placed side by side. The further away from one another, the less the impact. Some of the high-rise stitches pick up light reflections and throw shadows which contribute to the surface interest of the design. It is a great advantage to understand the various qualities inherent in the stitches you choose in order to get the maximum decorative mileage out of them. Tonal variations affect texture; the ranges of light and dark sprinkled over the composition vitalize it while introducing contrast. Light reveals the texture, especially as a stitch and thread changes direction. The amount is affected by the twists and turns the stitch takes.

Threads of different weights and fibers are the important sources of texture in embroidery. Yarns can be furry like angora, scratchy like jute, smooth as silk and rayon, nubby like chenille. A carefully considered mix of a few of these marvelous textures will bring enchanting contrasts and interest to embroidery design. Bulky, opaque threads placed next to fine, lustrous metallics will create a striking combination as one will dazzle in contrast to the other, allowing subdued and highlighted areas of design. The difference in scale of these two threads will affect the visual texture. Some of the natural handspun yarns are particularly worthy of notice for their provocative, uneven, grimy, hairy quality. Lightweight copper and aluminum wire are smooth, highly reflective materials that dazzle the eye, they are so reflective. Plastics and surgical tubing add relief to an otherwise flat surface to vary it. As always, I urge searching examination of any and all materials and objects in order to understand and control their marvelous and unique properties and effects. Recycled scrap materials, manufactured things, mentioned earlier, may be utilized for distinctive surface flavor as well as for the meaning they have as an image or symbol. The interplay between chicken wire and amber beads or washers and gold threads is extraordinarily engaging. Here you can visualize humble and rich, high and flat, quiet and gyrating effects, all together in a single design. It can be invention at its best, or worst if not done with taste and restraint.

Appliqué and collage fragments can be pleated, folded and gathered to intensify the high relief as the design is shaped. Almost three-dimensional, appliqué and collage techniques produce highly tactile surfaces. Suede, fur, plastics, corrugated paper are a few of the materials that can be superimposed on a textile background

Top: Angora, Danish cotton flower thread, bulky knitting wool, chenille, heavy angora, rayon ribbon, pearl cotton, Lurex, gold fingering metallic viscose thread, rayon metallic, metallic, tweeded nubby knitting yarn, DMC stranded cotton.

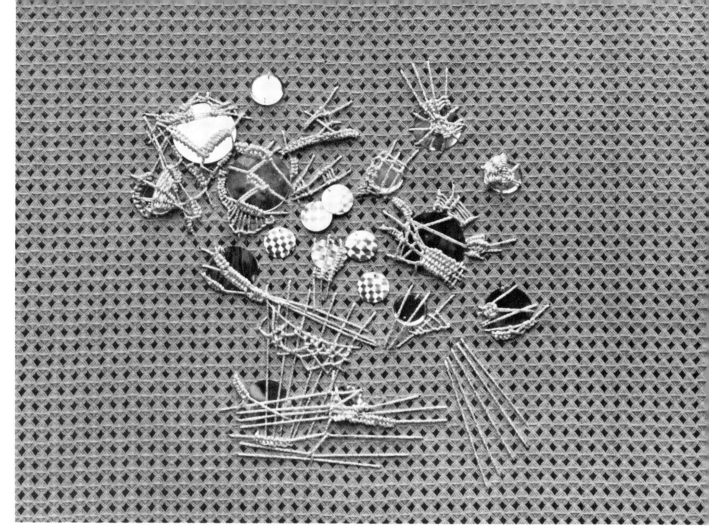

A Troll's Nosegay
The beginning stages of attaching round mirrors, silver paillettes to patterned pink straw. Some of the circles were later covered with silver thread and much design detail built from this point. Note the tiny diamond in the background fabric and the feeling of stripe in the weave. The circle form against this pattern and shape is a especially good. It is also fascinating that some of the mirrors look dark while some appear to be white, all stemming from the way light struck them. Whipped and woven stitches are combined with buttonhole stitches, freely worked. See color section.

for design purposes and tactile interest. Torn, frayed, curled, singed and fringed edges contribute to surface character. Whatever texture you introduce to embroidery, do so because it is urgent to the design scheme. Try to plan so that all design elements work in harmony, support each other and point to an area of primary interest. Too many textures can confuse and obscure the design, while none at all may result in monotony and lifelessness. Nature points the way in her landscape variation: smooths, roughs, highs, lows, ragged, rippled, even, irregular, light and dark all in proportion with taste.

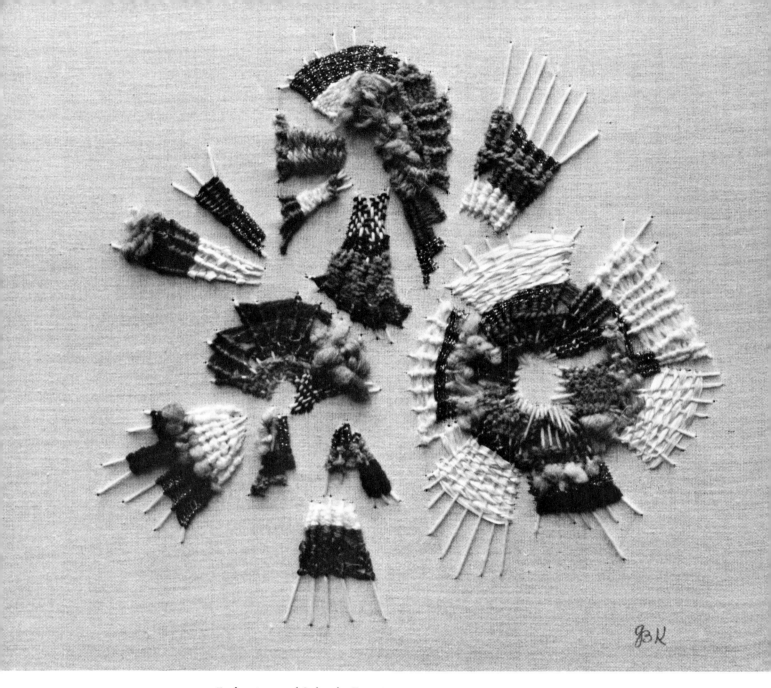

Early stage of Seismic Event
A view of the design as it gradually develops, taking turns and going in directions not yet certain. Notice whipped and woven straight stitches. See color section. Small motifs seem to dance or revolve around a large woven circle like recurrent explosions or sparks in various stages of activity. Rusts, salmons, beiges, coral, brown and white in straw, wool, ribbon and chenille threads compose the design. Amber glass beads are stitched between motifs to unify the whole, particularly as the design is fragmented. The beads as well as the lustrous straw threads reflect the light and move the eye around the composition.

Ivy-Stones Texture

Water-washed pebbles overlapped on needlepoint canvas cast marvelous shadows for design and reflect light in varying amounts to enliven the surface. The contrast between the smooth stones and the squared rough meshes of the canvas make the materials excellent partners in design.

In their natural setting, the pebbles team up with ivy in a less dramatic contrast. There are weeds and dried leaves that fill the spaces around the materials, all of different surface quality and of interest to the designer.

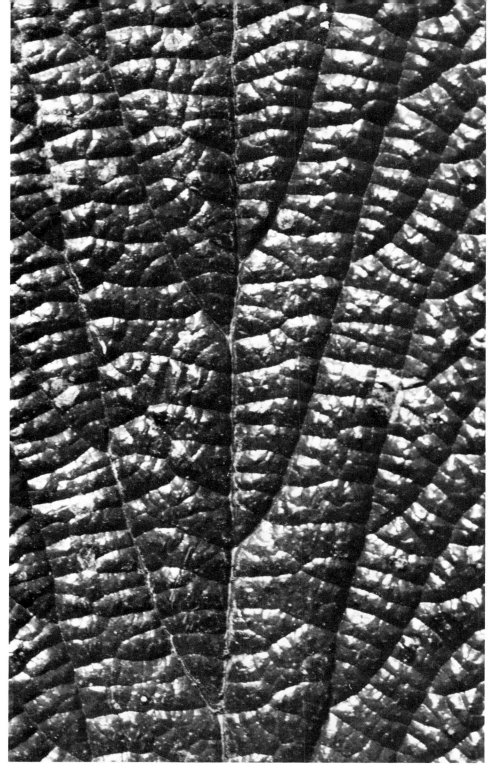

Texture
The viburnum leaf is heavily veined and so puckered that it looks quilted. Most interesting is the way it picks up and reflects fragments of light. The surface glistens yet has dark, matte areas and endless tiny creases between long curved and branching lines.

5

Blocking, Mounting and Finishing

The finishing, mounting and presentation of finished stitchery is as important as design and materials. Clumsy and careless finishing can destroy design when its purpose ought to be to complement it. On work that has been stretched preparatory to stitching, there is rarely distortion and puckering, therefore no need for later blocking; the design, when finished, can be considered mounted. A frame can be added to the work if needed or wanted as a finishing touch. A fabric not stretched at the start and worked in the hand will probably require blocking to restore the original shape and smooth out creases, folds and puckers. If you want the embroidery to hang softly, hem top and bottom of the work and insert a wood or metal or plexiglass rod, slat or dowel into the hems. The bottom will be weighted down by any one of these.

Padded, stuffed and shaped designs are also softly mounted, that is, not stretched taut. When the stitchery is finished, block, then cut away excess fabric, leaving just enough seam allowance (¼ inch) to attach the backing fabric which should be cut to fit the shape and size of the piece. Stitch the backing halfway around the wrong side of the design by hand or machine, leaving an opening in the other half through which to insert the filling. I use 100 per cent polyester fiber filling which I spread around as I want it, then tack in place so it won't move later. Close the remaining open area

101

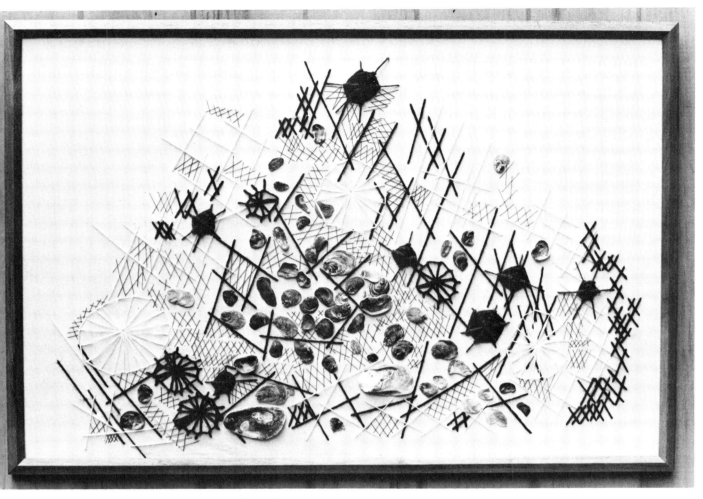

Squibnocket scape
Gray shells are glued to white duck fabric and surrounded with cross, button-hole, herringbone and spider web stitches, all reminiscent of images seen at the edge of the sea. Wool, cotton and straw threads are used in black, gray and deep burgundy. A narrow wood frame encircles the work.

with tiny invisible stitches. The design can be hung on the wall by means of one or two small rings attached to the backing. See Mod Mum.

Completed stitchery not pre-stretched can be later stapled to homosote or taped around masonite, carefully pulling fabric taut as you secure each of the four sides. The turned-under sides in all types of mounting can be covered with masking or mystic tape to give the underside a neat finish.

I never pre-stretch needlepoint before starting but work it in the hands, rolling or crushing to facilitate stitching; it always needs blocking, therefore. Because I use so many types of thread that would not withstand soaking in water, I have devised a mini blocking method. I simply dampen, not wet the entire unworked area around the embroidery and quickly staple or tack the damp canvas

Straight Op

This design is based on dividing needlepoint canvas into two parts by a diagonal line. One part is worked first with upright straight stitches in black and white alternately, in even horizontal rows, stopping at the diagonal line. The second side is worked afterward, the two sides joining up at the diagonal line where the colors are reversed to create the optical effect. A tent stitch border was added later and stitched with iridescent beads so that a mat surrounds the design. It is mounted against a shiny, black vinyl fabric to give it a finishing touch.

on a stretcher frame, pulling it tightly and evenly until perfectly smooth and straight. It dries rapidly on the frame without a sign of distortion. Be certain that the meshes of the canvas line up straight and the corners are mitered flat as you staple. I recommend lining needlepoint by stretching natural linen on the frame first. Never put any needlework under glass or its most distinguishing feature will be lost; the marvelous texture should be uncovered and exposed to the touch and the eye. Sign and date your designs unobtrusively at the bottom.

For final framing which is optional, I suggest professional advice and skill, though you should be able to do blocking and stretching at home. Before going to the framer, tidy up, clip loose threads and be sure the work is smooth, clean and even. A tastefully finished and framed embroidery will compel attention and stir imagination. See WEATHERED WOOD (p. 15). The frame should take into account the size, scale of the design, colors, texture and positioning of the composition on the background fabric. There can then be harmony between all parts, including the frame, which must never be over-elaborate, out of tune with the design or distracting. If your design is to function as a folding screen, seek the best professional help available, perhaps before you even start, so that all perils and pitfalls are anticipated.

Cloister scene
A graceful and provocative scene, nature is the backdrop to the curvy cobblestone walk which is outlined by a group of stanchions or posts. linked by swags of chains. The bold, black tree forms make an interesting contrast to the stone area, softening the composition.

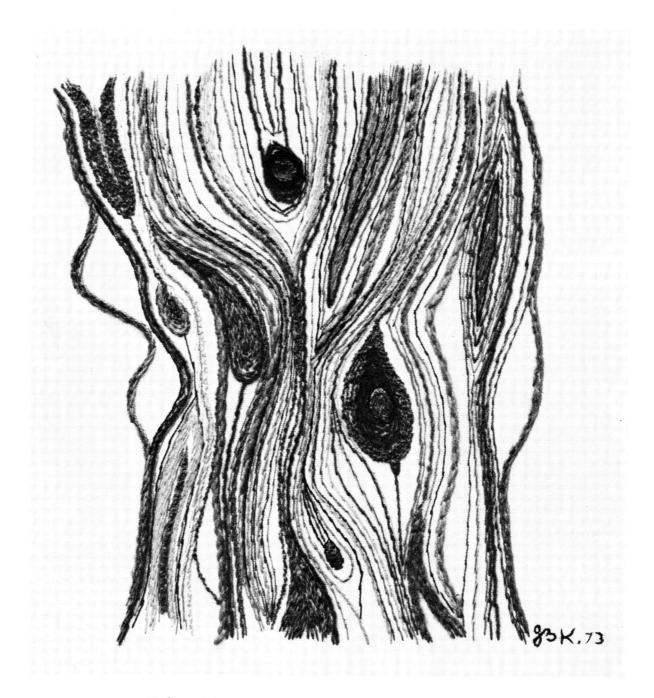

Bark swatch
Elaborated study of textures, color and movement based on knothole. The stem stitch conveys the graceful sway and swerve of the patterns and structure of bark and knots.

Bibliography

Art as the Measure of Man, George D. Stoddard, Museum of Modern Art, New York, 1964.

Creative Drawing . . . Point and Line, Ernst Rottger and Dieter Klante, B. T. Batsford, London, England, 1964.

Design in Embroidery, Kathleen Whyte, B. T. Batsford, Ltd., London, England, 1969.

Embroidery and Fabric Collage, Eirian Short, Charles Scribners' Sons, New York, 1971.

Ideas for Canvaswork, Mary Rhodes, B. T. Batsford, Ltd., London, England, 1970.

Inspiration for Embroidery, Constance Howard, B. T. Batsford, Ltd., London, England, 1966.

Interaction of Color, Joseph Albers, Yale University Press, New Haven, Connecticut, 1963.

On Weaving, Anni Albers, Wesleyan University Press, Middletown, Connecticut, 1965.

Needlework As Art, Lady M. Alford, Gilbert and Rivington, Ltd., London, England, 1886.

Needleweaving, Edith John, B. T. Batsford, Ltd., London, England, 1970.

Stitchery . . . Art and Craft, Nik Krevitsky, Reinhold Publishing Company, New York, 1966.

The Creative Process, edited by Brewster Ghiselin, University of California Press, Berkeley, California, 1952.

Wall Hangings . . . Designing with Fabric and Thread, Sarita R. Rainey, Davis Publications, Inc., Worcester, Massachusetts, 1971.

Wall Hangings of Today, Vera Sherman, Mills and Boon, Ltd., London, 1972.

Suppliers

Use yellow pages of local telephone books for fabric, yarns, framers, hardware stores.

NEW YORK
Yarns and Threads:
Alice Maynard, 558 Madison Avenue, Catalogue available.
Bloomingdale's, Lexington Avenue at 60th Street, mail order.
Boutique Margot,, 26 West 54th Street, mail order.
Fibre Yarn Company, Inc., 840 Sixth Avenue, mail order.
Tinsel Trading Company, 7 West 36th Street.
Yarn Center, 868 Sixth Avenue, Catalogue available.

Beads, Sequins, Trimmings:
Sheru, 49 West 38th Street, mail order.
Walbead, 38 West 37th Street, catalogue available.

Plastics:
Industrial Plastics Supply, 309 Canal Street.
Mail Order Plastics, 58 Lispenard Street, Catalogue available.

LONDON
Yarns and Threads:
The Needlewoman, 146 Regent Street.
Harrods', Brompton Road, Knightsbridge.
Dickins and Jones, Regent Street.

Beads, Sequins, Stones:
Ells and Farrier, 5 Princes Street.
The Bead Shop, 53 South Molton Street.